Refuge Denied

Refuge Denied

The St. Louis *Passengers and the Holocaust*

Sarah A. Ogilvie
and
Scott Miller
United States Holocaust
Memorial Museum

THE UNIVERSITY OF WISCONSIN PRESS

The University of Wisconsin Press
1930 Monroe Street, 3rd Floor
Madison, Wisconsin 53711-2059
uwpress.wisc.edu

3 Henrietta Street
London WC2E 8LU, England
eurospanbookstore.com

5   4

Printed in the United States of America

Library of Congress Cataloging-in-Publication Data
Ogilvie, Sarah A.
    Refuge denied: the St. Louis passengers and the Holocaust /
    Sarah A. Ogilvie and Scott Miller.
        p.   cm.
    Includes bibliographical references and index.
    ISBN 0-299-21980-1 (cloth: alk. paper)
        1. Jews—Germany—Biography.   2. St. Louis (Ship)
3. Holocaust, Jewish (1939-1945)—Biography.   4. Jews, German—Biography.
5. Refugees, Jewish—Biography.   6. Holocaust survivors—Biography.
7. Jews—Germany—History—1933-1945.   I. Miller, Scott, 1958-   II. Title.
DS135.G5A156   2006
940.53´180922—dc22   2006007518

ISBN 978-0-299-21984-0 (pbk.: alk. paper)

Contents

Illustrations

Museum Director's Foreword

As America's national steward of Holocaust history and memory, the United States Holocaust Memorial Museum is, in essence, a museum about responsibility: our responsibility to the past and to the memory of victims and survivors, our responsibility to our fellow human beings in the present, and—perhaps most important—our responsibility to future generations. Because of this, the Museum has a special interest in exploring those aspects of Holocaust history in which the government and people of the United States played direct roles, for good or ill. Such scholars as Arthur Morse and David Wyman have written with great eloquence about American indifference to the plight of European Jews during the 1930s and 1940s. As each of these writers has pointed out, to the extent that America did little to respond, it shares in the burden of the world's responsibility for allowing the Holocaust to happen.

No event is more emblematic of American apathy than the turning back of the Hamburg-America Line's MS *St. Louis* in June 1939. With this in mind, the Museum—in the persons of Sarah Ogilvie, director of the National Institute for Holocaust Education, and Scott Miller, director of the Benjamin and Vladka Meed Registry of Holocaust Survivors—endeavored to trace the fates of the more than nine hundred German Jewish passengers on that ship who, having seen the lights of Miami, were subsequently forced to return to Europe. Spanning ten years, Ogilvie and Miller's investigations have taken them from Los Angeles to Havana, from New York to Jerusalem. What is more, their quest has brought them into personal contact with nearly every living

Mechel and Lea Blumenstock with their infant daughter Ruth on the deck of the
St. Louis. (USHMM, courtesy of Ruth B. Mandel)

survivor of the *St. Louis* as well as dozens of family members and
descendents and yielded a rich cornucopia of stories. One story
was already well known to us, that of Ruth Blumenstock Mandel, the former vice chair of the Museum's governing board, who
made the journey as an infant and whose family photographs
of that fateful trip are on display in the Museum's permanent
exhibition.

The research done by Ogilvie and Miller shows that the fates
of the *St. Louis* passengers reflect the range of experiences of
other German Jews during the Holocaust. A total of 620 passengers were forced to return to the European mainland—288 of
their fellow travelers having been fortunate enough to be sent
to Britain. Of the passengers sent to Belgium, France, and the
Netherlands, 254 died during the Holocaust, including entire
families and children as young as six.

As a living memorial, the Museum is proud to present this
story, which reminds us that lessons of the Holocaust are both
timeless and timely.

SARA J. BLOOMFIELD
Director, United States Holocaust Memorial Museum

Foreword

The sad saga of the MS *St. Louis* was one of the first things I learned about America's response to the Holocaust. I do not remember precisely when I heard about it—it might have been in *While Six Million Died* by Arthur Morse (1968)—but the tragedy of the 937 passengers who were so close to safety and yet so far away was something that left me transfixed. I found myself imagining what it must have been like to have enjoyed the amenities of a first-class cruise ship and thought that you had escaped the Nazis' brutal hand, only to have it all snatched away.

When I began to teach about the Holocaust in general and America's response in particular, I always cited the saga of the *St. Louis* as an example of America's coldheartedness. Later, as I developed a more nuanced understanding of the period, I understood the constraints faced by American officials—there were many other ships crossing the Atlantic at the same time as the *St. Louis* and there were many people on the lists waiting for permission to enter the United States whose quota numbers were ahead of those on the *St. Louis.* Yet each time I used this example, I thought about the passengers lined up at the ship's railing close enough to see the lights of Miami. Certainly some exception to the rule could have been made.

Whenever I taught about this episode in history I always concluded with the comment that, except for those passengers who were lucky enough to be sent to the United Kingdom, most of the other passengers were certainly caught up in the jaws of the Nazi murder machine. "We will," I generally added, "never really know."

Irrespective of what we think of America's action, we now know that the statement "we will never really know" what happened to the other passengers is simply wrong. With the publication of this book the final stage in the saga of these very unlucky passengers has been rescued from oblivion. While some of them miraculously managed to escape once again, others ended up in gas chambers or were killed in other ways.

Despite the tragic subject of their investigations, the authors' work demonstrates the historians' thrill of the chase. In their methodical search to find the fate of each and every passenger, they relied on the internet and cutting-edge computer technology. As staff members at the United States Holocaust Memorial Museum, they had access to a multiplicity of archives and the most advanced computer search engines. But all was not so glamorous. They also engaged in gumshoe detective work. They checked burial society records, visited neighborhoods where German Jewish immigrants used to live, made phone calls to people with names similar to those on the ship, and put ads in German language newspapers. They trekked up the steps of buildings where people with names similar to passengers on the *St. Louis* once lived and spent countless hours in libraries—from the Library of Congress to New York's Forty-second Street mecca of old phone books.

Anyone who has wondered how historians do their research, how they piece together a story, will find an amazing tale in this book. It is one of hard work, creative thinking, dogged determination, and a deep commitment to leaving no passenger out.

One can sense Ogilvie and Miller's excitement as the results of their detective work allow them to tick each name off their list. However, the reader also grasps that they never lose sight of the fact that they are researching the fate of people, many of whom were murdered despite having been but a few miles from safety.

This is an exciting tale about a tragic story. Until Ogilvie and Miller did their research it was a tragic story without an end. The final chapter in the story of the MS *St. Louis* has now been written. And the passengers—both those who survived and those who died—now have their memorial.

DEBORAH LIPSTADT

Dorot Professor of Modern Jewish and Holocaust Studies, Emory University

Preface

We came to work together on the *St. Louis* project as two very different individuals with widely contrasting skills, abilities, and interests. Sarah, a native Virginian who is not Jewish, likes details and pored over long lists of names on the off chance of finding the smallest clue or lead. Scott, who is Jewish and a proud New Yorker by birth, was a natural networker who never sits still and was happiest using connections with people and organizations around the globe to advance our work.

We found over time that we complement each other and that in fact we have more in common than we first expected. We are of the same generation, longtime employees of the Holocaust Museum, children of fathers who fought in World War II, and clearly we share an unfulfilled yearning to do detective work. Collaborating as a team on a project and writing a book together are two different undertakings, however. We ultimately decided to tell the story of our search and the passengers we tracked down in the third person, after many drafts in which we unsuccessfully attempted to weave together a complicated narrative in first-person voice. Trying to relate our experiences directly meant spilling a great deal of ink in order to keep straight who was doing what with whom at what point in time—all tangential to what we felt was the real story. Using the third person is not a perfect solution, but it is one that we hope allows the passengers' stories to come to the fore.

Since the whole purpose of our work was to trace all of the passengers' experiences, one of the hardest parts of writing this book was deciding which stories to include. We have tried to be balanced in representing geography, fate, and different ages and genders. However, we could not have done justice to the wide range of experiences that include: men who enlisted in the U.S. Army and helped liberate Europe from the Nazis; the first American soldier released in a prisoner exchange with Korea in 1953; a woman who was born in Ankara, Turkey; a man who left wartime Europe a second time for Cuba and is buried outside of Havana; two brothers who unknowingly left the relative safety of England and headed home to Romania and an uncertain future; and a husband and wife who, if alive today, would be 140 and 134 years old, respectively.

Finally, a note about place names. We have tried as much as possible to cite the name of each place in the text in the language of the country or entity it was located in at the time. Exceptions include places for which there is an accepted English-language version. Where concentration camps, killing centers, and other places of internment are concerned, we have used the German names.

Acknowledgments

This book would never have been possible without the support and contributions of hundreds of individuals. Sheila Johnson Robbins, a two-time presidential appointee to the United States Holocaust Memorial Council and longtime Museum friend, deserves special acknowledgment. She has been part of the *St. Louis* project from the beginning, encouraging us all along the way. Sheila, it is because of you that this story can finally be told.

The effort to trace the passengers began ten years ago, not long after the Holocaust Museum opened its doors to the public. We thank Michael Berenbaum and Radu Ioanid for creating a work environment in those early days in which a project such as this one could flourish. Over the past ten years we received generous assistance and support from *St. Louis* survivors as well as their relatives, friends, and neighbors from all over the world. Too numerous to name, these individuals provided information that was often not available from any other sources; without them the effort to trace all of the passengers would most certainly have fallen short.

Only one staff member has been involved with the project continuously since the beginning. Michael Haley Goldman has supported the research effort and writing of this book in countless ways: through his creative database design, oversight of volunteers, troubleshooting of snags along the way, and not least through his enthusiasm and unwavering commitment and patience with last minute requests. It has been an honor to work with you, Michael.

Salif Nimaga from the German organization Action Reconcil-iation Service for Peace, with assistance from then high school student Kadian Pow, made a critical contribution at the begin-ning, becoming an avid detective after four *St. Louis* survivors visited the Museum in 1996. They laid the groundwork for all that was to come.

Survivors Registry staff, volunteers, and interns have served as the backbone of the project for the duration. Peter Lande pro-vided both perspiration and inspiration, feeding us with leads and advice and doing painstaking work to digitize the many lists of names we used as sources. David Wigmore and Danielle Henry pored over blurry concentration camp records and interviewed survivors on the phone. Vadim Altskan assisted with a major re-view of our case files and willingly took over tasks from others to free up their time to work on the *St. Louis* project. Georg Echtler, another Action Reconciliation Service for Peace intern, followed leads for us in Germany, conducted interviews, and has always been an energetic supporter. William Connelly, Steven Vitto, and Megan Lewis followed the trail on specific cases, suggested new avenues of research, assisted with vetting of place names, and have generally shown their support in ways too numerous to count. Pavel Ilyin lent his expertise in geography and helped us polish the final draft of the manuscript. Many Registry volun-teers were responsible for digitizing lists of names and other labo-rious tasks that made our search possible, including Ina Altman, David Bayer, Dan Lednicer, Henry Brauner, Phyllis Goldberg, Carol Jones, Joan Kahn, Norm Kaufman, Mel Meltzer, Abe Muhl-baum, Rita Permut, Gloria Simon, Ted Smith, and Ed Weiner.

As the *St. Louis* project gained momentum, the circle of Mu-seum staff involved grew. We will always be grateful to Shana Penn, who recognized the power of the story early on and played a pivotal role in enlisting the media in our search. Mary Morri-son, former head of communications, gave us critical guidance, and director of media relations Andy Hollinger offered further tips, coaching us through any number of radio, print, and televi-sion interviews. Christine Brown of the External Affairs Office coached us for our media and public presentations throughout the duration of the search project. Legal counsels Stuart Bender and Ronald Cuffe advised us on copyright issues and were al-ways eager for updates on the project's progress.

Researchers in the Wexner Learning Center joined the team to help us trace the final hundred passengers. Etan Kelman never gave up on the toughest cases, doggedly trying new approaches until the National Archives finally yielded answers. Andy Wackerfuss reminded us not to overlook our own collections, revisiting the Museum's holdings to resolve several passengers' stories and searching the internet to find family connections. Cindy DeGesero believed in this project, helping with almost every aspect from research to fact checking, to entering addresses in our database. Ralph Grunewald, former director of external affairs, reached out to archives and Jewish organizations in Europe, South America, and other far-flung locales.

Historians throughout the Museum have offered their expertise and support at critical junctures. Senior historian Peter Black provided key insights about German records as well as the holdings of the International Tracing Service. Martin Dean guided us to a number of important clues in restitution records. Keith Allen followed leads for us in Europe, as did Jürgen Matthäus. Klaus Mueller went the extra mile to locate documentation in Dutch archives and was responsive to every request, no matter how detailed. Severin Hochberg and Steven Luckert painstakingly reviewed this manuscript, correcting any number of errors and helping us understand the difference between viewing the *St. Louis* story from today's vantage point versus the way it was seen at the time. William Meinecke provided endless translations and professional advice, always with patience and good cheer. Timothy Kaiser provided on-the-spot translations during the final stages of the project.

Peggy Frankston from the International Programs Division pursued numerous leads in France, where both Polly Haas, a volunteer for the Museum's Oral History project, and Museum fellow Diane Afoumado did the legwork necessary to tie up a few of the final unresolved cases.

Outreach Technology staff Larry Swiader, Adele O'Dowd, Sandra Kaiser, and David Klevan built a beautiful website documenting the story of the *St. Louis* and provided another outlet for people to contact us with leads. Media specialist Josh Blinder was an unflagging supporter, filming interviews with survivors and helping us see the potential in the story of the search.

Staff in our Collections Department offered many leads and

regularly followed up with passengers and their family members to acquire artifacts, photographs, and documents. Thank you Sharon Muller, Judy Cohen, Teresa Pollin, and Lisa Toppelman. Suzy Snyder worked tirelessly to encourage survivors and family members to entrust the Museum with their materials. Ferenc Katona assisted us with research in Hungary and served as translator on a number of occasions. Joan Ringelheim made professional oral histories possible for a number of passengers and has provided invaluable moral support and advice about publishing our work. Finally, Genya Markon ably served as photo editor for this work. She embraced the task with great enthusiasm and successfully expanded our collection of *St. Louis* photographs through her sensitive and caring contact with survivors and their family members.

Under the leadership of Stephen Goodell, our exhibitions staff created *Voyage of the* St. Louis, a special exhibition curated by Steven Luckert and Suzy Snyder marking the sixtieth anniversary of the ship's voyage. Its success and visibility generated even more leads for our search. Meanwhile, Kristine Donly coordinated *St. Louis*-related programming around the exhibition, helping us keep things together during a particularly hectic time.

Two exceptionally talented individuals came to work at the Museum as a result of the *St. Louis* project. Elizabeth Hedlund read an article in the *Washington Post* in 1998 and called to volunteer her services. Elizabeth conducted interviews with family members, returned hundreds of phone calls and e-mails that came in following major media stories, and, perhaps most important, helped us put order in our files. Molly Abramowitz lent her considerable skills as a professional editor/indexer as well as her unparalleled internet and sleuthing abilities in the latter phases of the project. Without Molly, there would no doubt still be unaccounted for passengers.

Sarah Hyams joined the project to assist with the final stages of the search and the verification of basic information about each passenger, bringing patience and attention to detail as well as great team spirit and passion for the project to an often tedious undertaking. Director of publishing Mel Hecker advocated for publishing a book to share the results of our research and has stood by our side through every draft and revision. Sometimes he wondered if we would ever finish, but he never gave up on us.

We are ever grateful to the leadership of the Museum, Director Sara Bloomfield as well as William Parsons, Arnold Kramer, and Alice Greenwald, for giving us time off from our regular job responsibilities to write this book as well as their ongoing support for documenting and sharing the stories of the *St. Louis* passengers.

In addition to our colleagues at the Museum, a number of very able researchers assisted us abroad. Shalom Bronstein did painstaking work in Jerusalem archives. Amy Gottlieb and David Fielker helped us fill in gaps on the passengers who went to England. Lutz Krätzschmar's research in France provided invaluable clues for resolving some of the most difficult cases. We have also benefited from the generous assistance of a long list of archives and other organizations around the globe: in Austria, Dokumentations archiv des Österreichischen Widerstandes; in Belgium, Me. Cl. Barette, Ministère des Affaires Sociales de la Santé Publique et de l'Environment, Ward Adriaens, Joods Museum von Deportatie; in Chile, Ram Tapia Adler, B'nai B'rith; in France, Jacques Fredj, Centre de Documentation Juif Contemporaine, Christine Diatta, Ministère des Anciens Combattants et Victims de Guerres; in Germany, Jean Claude Biedermann, International Tracing Service, I.A. Ledermann, Jewish community, Magdeburg, Arno Hamburger, Jewish community, Nürnberg, Barbara Distel, KZ-Gedenkstätte Dachau; Stiftung Neue Synagogue Berlin; in Israel, Alex Avraham, Yad Vashem, Sara Kadosh, American Jewish Joint Distribution Committee archive in Jerusalem, Alisah Schiller, Beit Theresienstadt, Batya Unterschatz, Jewish Agency's Missing Persons Bureau; in Italy, Liliana Picciotto Fargione, Fondazione Centro di Doumentazione Ebraica Contemporanea; in the Netherlands, Herinneringscentrum kamp Westerbork, Peter Buijs, Jewish Historical Museum, Rabbi Dr. Tzvi Marx, B. Folkertsma Institute for Talmudica; in Poland, Jerzy Wróblewski, Pan'stwowe Muzeum Auschwitz-Birkenau; in Switzerland, Bundesarchiv; in the United States, Eric Nooter, American Jewish Joint Distribution Committee, Brad Silver, Jewish Community Council of the Bronx, Marian Smith and David Cunningham, U.S. Immigration and Naturalization Service Office of Records, Miriam Bowling, New York Public Library and Gunner Berg, YIVO Institute for Jewish Research.

Finally, doing research is one thing, writing a book for public consumption entirely another. We would likely still be floundering with an unfinished manuscript were it not for the assistance of Edward J. Renehan Jr., who did yeoman's work in helping us massage our prose into readable form.

Sarah Ogilvie and Scott Miller

Washington, D.C., January 2006

Refuge Denied

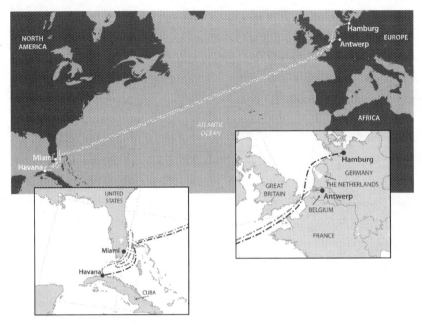

The voyage of the *St. Louis*, May/June 1939. (USHMM)

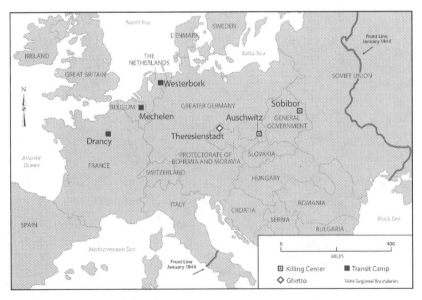

Major sites where *St. Louis* passengers were interned or deported, including ghettos and killing centers. (USHMM)

Introduction

During the last week of May 1939, the government of Cuba officially refused to grant entry to more than nine hundred Jews fleeing Hitler's Germany. The people in question were passengers aboard the Hamburg-America Line's MS (Motor Ship) *St. Louis.* Previous boatloads of refugees had successfully found sanctuary in Havana. But now, quite suddenly, a convergence of factors—including greed, political infighting, public agitation against immigration, fascist influences, and anti-Semitism (a mix to be detailed elsewhere in this volume)—changed that equation, making the majority of those aboard the *St. Louis* unwelcome on Cuban soil.

Shortly thereafter, the German liner cruised within sight of Miami, where Captain Gustav Schröder was barred from making port. Several U.S. Coast Guard cutters surrounded the vessel to make sure that none of the would-be émigrés attempted to swim for shore.

Most of the *St. Louis's* passengers had already applied for United States visas. They had intended to stay in Cuba only until such time as their numbers came up on Bureau of Immigration and Naturalization quota lists. Despite this, appeals to President and Mrs. Franklin Delano Roosevelt that referenced the persecution the refugees would encounter should they be returned to Germany went unanswered. Facing repatriation, the *St Louis* passengers openly discussed the possibility of mass suicide.

Finally, on June 12, after many days of negotiations, the American Jewish Joint Distribution Committee (JDC) brokered a solution. Several European countries other than Germany agreed to take in the 908 passengers forced to return to Europe. Although 288 refugees wound up in Britain, the balance (except for Istvan Winkler, who was not a refugee at the time) went to the Netherlands, Belgium, and France and to uncertain fates in a Europe about to be overrun by Hitler.

The *St. Louis* affair has come to symbolize the world's indifference to the plight of European Jewry on the eve of World War II. The episode speaks directly to contradictions in American society when it was faced with the increasingly alarming effects of Hitler's totalitarian regime. On the one hand, there was widespread disapproval of Nazi brutality and persecution of Jews and other minorities. On the other hand, tough economic times, isolationism, and anti-Semitism hindered any moves to let more refugees in. In the end, the resulting gap—"between sympathy and action"—proved too great to overcome.

No study of United States policy and politics during the Holocaust can ever be complete without a full understanding of the *St. Louis* story: not just the events of late May and early June 1939 but also what happened afterward to the hundreds of desperate men, women, and children. Under the auspices of the United States Holocaust Memorial Museum, Sarah and Scott have worked since 1996 to track the fates and resurrect the stories of the *St. Louis* passengers. *Refuge Denied* presents the fruits of this quest.

Refuge Denied is dedicated to the families, past and present, of the *St. Louis*. With reference to the greatest number of passengers, this book is intended to serve as a testament to the capacity of individuals to endure in the face of injustice. With reference to the balance, *Refuge Denied* will have to serve as something else altogether: an act of witness to terrible, senseless loss.

1

A Mystery Beckons

Dr. Clark Blatteis—a distinguished, gray-haired physiologist associated with the University of Tennessee College of Medicine—paced the United States Holocaust Memorial Museum one warm spring day in April 1996. The serious, soft-spoken doctor had a certain look, a particular gait and demeanor of the type that veteran Museum staffers had come to recognize. There were many who visited every day simply as tourists. But there were others who arrived with a different purpose. These were pilgrims with a sense of mission. These were searchers intent on rediscovering and giving witness to their turbulent and troubled past. As for Dr. Blatteis, any Museum employee worth his or her salt would have instantly, and correctly, figured him for a pilgrim and searcher rather than a sightseer.

Walking the sometimes narrow and frequently dark halls of the Museum's exhibition space, Blatteis passed greatly enlarged photographs taken at Buchenwald and Dachau. Uniformed prisoners stared out with blank, lifeless eyes. Blatteis returned their gaze, glad his father was not among them. After all, Ernst (Elias) Blatteis—shoe salesman and once-proud Berliner—had endured and then risen from both these terrible places, hadn't he? In the end, Ernst (Elias) had not only emerged from the camps but had gone on with his wife, Gerda, and his young son to make a life in the United States—a land that at first had wanted nothing to do with them.

Blatteis paused for an especially long time at the Museum's exhibit showcasing the story of the German liner *St. Louis*. Designed quite purposely to be tight and claustrophobic, thus mimicking the narrowing of options experienced by German Jews during the late 1930s, the display dedicated to the *St. Louis* sat wedged in a narrow corner on one of the Museum's upper floors. The exhibit used contemporary newspaper articles, passenger belongings, and original documents together with cutting-edge multimedia to deliver a condensed rendition of the *St. Louis* saga.

The photos at the start of the corridor presented placid, unremarkable scenes of a typical luxury voyage. Antique black-and-white images depicted young couples playing shuffleboard, grandparents lounging in deck chairs, happy children cavorting, and stylish women sipping champagne at formal dinners. Blatteis also viewed relatively ordinary artifacts, including the hat once worn by Captain Gustav Schröder.

Farther down the dark hall, however, the display turned ominous. Several old newspaper photos, greatly enlarged, showed the desperate scene in Havana harbor. Small boats crowded with relatives and friends circled the sequestered *St. Louis.* Still more vessels—police boats standing as "suicide guards"—hovered even closer. Near the newspaper photos, a glass case housed the original telegram from *St. Louis* passengers addressed to the wife of Federico Bru, president of Cuba, pleading the case of women and children aboard the vessel.

Clark Blatteis had himself been one of those children.

Thus, later that same day in the Museum's well-lighted, library-like room housing the Benjamin and Vladka Meed Registry of Jewish Holocaust Survivors, he took his quest for the past one step further. Launched in 1981 by the American Gathering of Holocaust Survivors (an organization founded by the Meeds, two survivors of the Warsaw ghetto), the Registry had been donated to the Museum in 1993. Survivors and family members come from all over the world to search the database for information about lost relatives. But, oddly, the Registry included hardly any of the names for which Blatteis sought information.[1]

After spending some unproductive time at the computers, Blatteis decided to try another tack. "My name is Clark Blatteis," he said, extending his hand to a young woman working at a nearby desk. "I was a passenger on the *St. Louis.* I'm looking for more information about my parents and some other passengers. Can you help me?"

Sarah Ogilvie had never planned for a career as a Holocaust researcher, curator, and educator. Nevertheless she had long nourished a deep interest in the great catastrophe imposed on European Jewry under the Nazis. She had grown up on tales told by her father, a World War II U.S. Army sergeant who once helped administer a displaced persons (DP) camp in Austria. "It was definitely a defining experience in his life," Sarah recalls.

> I was captivated by his stories. I guess it's also important to note that my father was a Presbyterian minister. A lot of our family dinners were spent discussing and dissecting big questions like "How could the Holocaust have happened?" Also, I was a high school student in 1978 when the television docudrama *The Holocaust* aired, stimulating discussion across the country and generating great interest on the part of students like me who had studied European history but had heard no mention of this cataclysmic event (in class at least). Apparently I was part of a wave of students who went to school the next day after the piece aired demanding to know more. There was a real element of "How can we consider these teachers to be credible if they're teaching us Western Civilization but omitting the one event that seems to make that an oxymoron?"

Much later, during two years in an interdisciplinary PhD program at Emory University, Sarah pursued in-depth studies of the Holocaust's various ramifications—economic and theological as well as historical.

By the summer of 1989, Sarah had long since settled for her master's and was living in Washington, D.C. Ironically, she was not even seriously looking for a job when, casually glancing through the *Washington Post,* she spotted an announcement for a research post at the fledgling United States Holocaust Memorial Museum, a position that sounded as though it had been custom designed for her. Sarah spent the next three and a half years helping develop what would become the Museum's permanent exhibition. Upon the opening of the Museum in April 1993, she received a promotion to deputy director of the Meed Registry, the position she still held when she found herself greeted by Clark Blatteis in 1996.[2]

Blatteis told Sarah he was especially hoping to find information concerning the fates of children with whom, as a seven-year-old, he had enjoyed high, happy times during the *St. Louis*'s journey. Most important, he was interested in finding the whereabouts of Rudi Jacobson, a boy with whom he had become very fast friends. He recalled how one day early in the trip, the two wound up in disgrace after hiding in a lifeboat when they should have been at dinner. By the time they reappeared, their parents and the *St. Louis*'s captain—fearing they had been lost overboard—had organized a search party and were busy scouring the ship. The boys were punished by their parents for inconveniencing the crew and their fellow passengers.

"Generally, I have memories of having had a lot of fun on the ship. I have no great recollection of the consternation that must have been felt by the older ones when we were not allowed to land. So either we, the younger ones, were shielded very well, or it didn't affect us. We were not understanding. I just remember running around and swimming in the pool and having a real nice time."[3] But Blatteis also recalled standing with his father at the ship's rail, looking at the lights of Miami, and hearing his father say that Florida's golden shore, so near, might as well be four thousand miles away for all the good it did them.

Although Blatteis had many other clear recollections, he had never discussed the *St. Louis* with his parents, a fact that he regretted after their deaths in the 1980s. Nor had he talked with them much about the troubles that afflicted the Blatteis family before and after that fateful journey. It was the outline of this story that Blatteis now shared with Sarah, thus supplying the first piece for a puzzle that she had not yet realized needed solving.

The Blatteis family of Berlin were Ashkenazi Jews, and not particularly religious. They celebrated the High Holy Days but did not regularly attend synagogue. (In later years, when young Clark reached the age of manhood, his parents did not even bother to have a bar mitzvah ceremony for him.) Religious or not, the Blatteis clan became targets of Nazi power in June 1938. During a sales trip to the eastern German town of Cottbus, Clark's father found himself placed under arrest—his only crime being his Jewish descent.

He was due to come back on Clark's birthday, June 25, 1938. "I remember particularly because one of my uncles gave me a gift of a record, and the record was 'The Toreador Song' from

				S.S. ST. LOUIS (TRISCORNIA)			
Surname	M.	W.		Maiden Name	Family Status		Case No.
BLATTEIS	ELIAS	GERDA					

ADDRESS Belgium

Relatives on S. S. St. Louis

	Date of					Registration with Consul		
1st Name	Birth	Nativity	Passport	Occupation	Date	Place	Waiting No.	
H Elias	2/15/00	Krakau		Vertreter		Berlin	14856	
W Gerda	9/14/00	Lunow/P				"	14857	
Ch Hans	6/15/29	Berlin				"	14858	
2.								
3.								

	Name	Address	Contact Through	Result of Contact
Affiants	Benjamin S. Blatteis 594 Lincoln Place Bklyn. N.Y.			
	Benjamin Blatteis 1096 Park Place Brooklyn, N.Y.			
Relatives in U. S.				
Relatives in Belgium				
England	S. Blatteis	London,150 Walm.Lane Cricklewood		
Holland	C. Bergmann	London W. 1, 8, Conduit Str.Regentatr.		
France				

Passenger registration card for the Blatteis family. (USHMM)

Carmen. I don't know if that has anything to do with my lifelong love of opera, but there it is, imprinted in my memory. There was a knock and my mother went to the door expecting to open it to my father, but instead two policemen were there. . . . A little while later, my mother went to visit him."

Clark's father was first put in a regular prison in Cottbus. Then, eventually, the SS moved him to Buchenwald and, after some months, to Dachau. "It was while he was in the concentration camp that my mother began the work to get us out of the country. And it was during that time that she, I guess, purchased the passes, these permits, for Cuba, where we could wait for our American visas to come up."

The shoe salesman Ernst (Elias) Blatteis was released only after his wife, Gerda, presented the Gestapo with the Blatteis family's visas for entry to Cuba together with their tickets for departure aboard the *St. Louis.* Meanwhile, Clark's education in German public schools had ended abruptly following Kristallnacht—November 9–10, 1938—with the Reich's November 15 announcement that Jewish children were no longer welcome at institutions of learning.

"I had been, during the time while my mother was busy making all these arrangements, moved to one of my grandmother's—my maternal grandmother's—and stayed with her." But soon the grandmother immigrated to Johannesburg, South Africa, where several other family members had already moved a few years before. "After she left I returned to my mother. Then my father was released—with a shaved head. I hardly recognized him. He joined us in Berlin, but then later my mother and I traveled to Hamburg, and the *St. Louis,* just the two of us by ourselves. My father came separately. There was a reason for this arrangement, but I forget now what it was. I do recall, however, that we boarded the ship together."

Likewise they disembarked together, at Antwerp, after the grave disappointment at Havana and the rejection off the coast of the United States. "We had hoped to be selected for England, because my grandparents, my father's parents, were there. But that didn't happen." The family eventually settled in an apartment in Brussels, where Clark resumed his schooling and used his knack for languages to pick up French very quickly. "I served as translator for my parents for quite some time, because it took them a whole lot longer. In fact, I don't think my father ever learned to speak French very well. But I did." Clark's mother, meanwhile, wasted no time in applying—actually reapplying, as they had already filed paperwork before the voyage of the *St. Louis*—for American visas.

World War II began in September 1939, but Belgium was not invaded until May 1940. "In Europe at those latitudes in the fair weather the nights are short. I think the Germans attacked at about four in the morning. And we heard *boom boom boom,* the anti-aircraft guns. I remember going to the window and seeing these little white puffs exploding in the air and planes way, way up. Then people came running from upper floors. They knocked on our door, and they were telling us that the Germans were bombing and that we had to go to the cellar, which we did. Soon the bombs began to fall. It was a very frightening noise. I remember I was very, very frightened."

There was a lot of destruction—not right where the Blatteis family lived but around them. Many of the windows in the Blatteis family's building were shattered by the explosions. "My father and I went out sometime later, maybe a day or two later, to see what had happened. And when we returned, my mother had been arrested as an enemy alien, a German, by the Belgian

authorities. We had to go try and get her. The Belgians had assembled all the German refugees in a school. It was not the
school to which I had been going but another one also nearby. So
we went in and we found my mother, and we were all three
interviewed and then released."

With the Germans in rapid advance, the only thing for Clark
and his parents to do was what everyone else was doing: head
south. They could not carry much, so most of what they owned
had to be left behind. As the German Wehrmacht (army) closed
in on the city, the Blatteis family joined the throng at the Brussels
train station, vainly attempting to board what was rumored to be
the last train leaving. "That train departed and it looked like
there wouldn't be another. Then we and many of the other refugees were thrown out of the station, and the station doors were
locked." With no other option, the family began walking south.
They had not gone far when, serendipitously, they encountered a
friendly Belgian soldier who informed them that another train
would depart shortly and that they should hike back to the
station along the railroad tracks so as to circumvent the locked
doors. "We made that second train, the true last train. And later,
when our train caught up with the previous one, we saw that it
had been bombed, and they, all the people on it, were dead and
wounded: a terrible scene."

Many of the passengers on the Blatteis's train disembarked
at Paris. "Nobody thought the Germans would ever get to Paris.
That city, for some reason, seemed safe. But my parents knew
no one in Paris, so we stayed on the train and continued south
to Toulouse near the town of Roques, where we spent about a
month, maybe two." Toulouse was pleasant enough at first, but
every day, as the Germans moved deeper and deeper into France,
it got more crowded. Nevertheless the camp remained a safe
place to be—at least for the moment. When France signed its surrender (euphemistically called an "armistice") on June 22, 1940,
the document set the demarcation line *north* of Roques. Thus
Clark and his parents were spared from falling into German
hands.

Clark recalled that he personally enjoyed life in Toulouse.
"There were lots of children to play with, and there were lots of
games. It was summer, and we were camping. But my parents
were wondering, of course, what to do next. We couldn't stay

there forever. Somebody suggested Morocco, which sounded very exotic, far away, and removed from difficulties. Of course, we needed to get visas to travel through Spain, because it was well known that the Spanish—unlike the authorities in some other countries—were arresting refugees traveling illegally. My mother was very ingenious in these things, and somehow she got the appropriate paperwork." Soon thereafter, Clark and his parents went by car with another couple up into to the Pyrenees, crossed into Spain, and then journeyed to Algerciras.

Clark and his parents crossed the Strait of Gibraltar on a ferry to Spanish Morocco and then traveled to French Morocco and beautiful, white Casablanca.[4] There the American Jewish Joint Distribution Committee (JDC) and a group of Moroccan Jews helped the Blatteis family find a small studio apartment, which was all they could afford. "My parents started me back at school immediately, and I attended the public school until the Vichy government expelled Jewish children from the schools. After that I went to a local Jewish school." Meanwhile, Clark's father, who had been a salesman all his life, now worked as a common laborer. He learned to cut leather for shoes. His wages were very low, but the family was able to pay its way.

"Every once in a while there would be a panic," Clark remembered. "Rumors would fly round that everyone, all we stateless refugees, all we people without nationalities, were going to be arrested." But it never happened. There were no German occupiers in Morocco, just a token force. "German submariners would often take their leaves in Morocco. They would be wearing civilian clothes, but you knew who they were. They recognized us, too, of course, and realized we were German Jews. But it is interesting, and maybe a bit odd, that they were never unpleasant or impolite. So it wasn't easy for us there, but it also wasn't that bad considering what was going on in other places."

Still, Clark and his parents were relieved to see the Americans arrive in 1942. "I left the Jewish school and went back to the French school after the Americans came and the Vichy were gone. Finally, in 1948, we got visas for the United States. You know, it is funny and it is sad. We were contacted after the war by the Germans, the new German government, inviting us back to Germany. Some people did go, but my parents had no interest.

Germany was over for them, and for me. I was sixteen when we came to the United States in 1948."

It was impossible to listen to Clark Blatteis's story without considering the vagaries of fate. Seemingly small questions—such as what train one happened to get on, which station one happened to get off at, and the random latitude of a dotted line drawn on an armistice map—could ultimately have quite large (in fact, life-or-death) consequences.

For the passengers of the *St. Louis*, selection for Britain had meant virtually guaranteed survival, whereas selection for the Netherlands, Belgium, or France meant continued risk once the Nazis overran those countries. Writing in his 1967 book *While Six Million Died*, Arthur Morse said that "the only *St. Louis* refugees protected from the Nazi terror were those who had found sanctuary in Britain. Many—it is impossible to know how many—died in the German gas chambers following the Nazi invasions of Belgium, Holland and France."[5] Seven years later, Gordon Thomas and Max Morgan-Witts echoed this sentiment in their 1974 bestseller *Voyage of the Damned*: "For many of the refugees on the *St. Louis*, their rescue proved to be the beginning of the end. [Those] who went to England were the luckiest. . . . No one can say with certainty how many of the *St. Louis* passengers eventually perished."[6] A 1976 movie based on the book (starring Faye Dunaway, Max Von Sydow, and Oskar Werner) ended with the same grim generalization. Yet here was a man sitting across from Sarah and bearing witness to the escape of his entire family. How many more *St. Louis* passengers got out alive? And how many did not? Compounding Sarah's question was the quirky fact—a coincidence?—that Clark Blatteis was the fourth *St. Louis* passenger to come into the Registry that week.

Listening to Dr. Blatteis narrate his family's utterly unique tale of survival, Sarah sensed that the largest part of the history of the *St. Louis* had yet to be researched and written. The ship's manifest—a part of the Museum collection that Sarah now allowed Blatteis to look at in its entirety—listed 937 passengers. Of that total, one passenger died en route to North America, 28 had been allowed to enter Cuba, 620 were returned to continental Europe, with 288 going to Britain. A passenger who attempted suicide in Havana harbor was initially hospitalized there but later joined his family in Britain. This meant that out there, somewhere, were hundreds of individual stories waiting to be uncovered, hundreds of human dramas that deserved—no, demanded—recognition. In short order, Sarah decided to do her best to track down the fate of each and every *St. Louis* refugee and to write the final chapter of the infamous voyage.

2

Fateful Voyage

D uring the morning of May 13, 1939, the Hamburg-America
Line's MS *St. Louis* departed Hamburg for Havana. On
the surface, the departure bore all the earmarks of normalcy. A
band played. Flags flew. Friends and families of the ship's passengers waved from the pier. The day held a great deal of exuber-
ance but also much sadness, as the 937 passengers, most of them
German Jews, realized they were leaving—probably forever—
the country that had been their home for all their lives. Not a
few of the men who hung onto the railing, taking a last look at
their fatherland, had been decorated heroes of the German army
during World War I. Up until recently, they had considered
themselves patriots, loyal and proud Germans. But now these
Jews—who had watched the Nazis systematically destroy their
neighborhoods, businesses, and synagogues—bid farewell to
their homeland with a strange mix of emotions, an odd intermin-
gling of regret and relief. But grief over leaving was, in the end,
washed away by the prospect of deliverance from harm's way.

The eight-decked vessel held room for more than four
hundred first-class passengers (at 800 Reichsmarks, about $320,
each) and more than five hundred tourist-class passengers (at
600 Reichsmarks, about $240, each).[1] The cost of every passen-
ger's ticket included a "contingency fee" of 230 Reichsmarks
(about $92) that was meant to protect the Hamburg-America
Line against losses should an unplanned return voyage become
necessary. Return, however, was on no one's mind as the *St. Louis*
steamed down the Elbe and then out into the calm waters of the
North Atlantic.

Members of the Hess and Heilbrun families board the *St. Louis* in the port of Hamburg. Left to right: Martin Hess, Vera Hess, Bruno Heilbrun, Ruth Heilbrun, and Sally Heilbrun. (USHMM, courtesy of Ruth Heilbrun Windmuller)

Postcard advertising the *St. Louis*, purchased aboard the ship by a member of the Dingfelder family. (USHMM, courtesy of Gerri Felder)

An evening on board the *St. Louis*. (USHMM, courtesy of Rolf Allen)

The weather seemed idyllic; so, too, did the tone and rhythm of the stately *St. Louis*—this at odds with the disrupted lives most passengers had experienced during recent months and years. Aboard the ship, men who had prior to this been prisoners at Dachau and Buchenwald, and who had been released only on their pledge to depart Germany promptly, were waited on by the *St. Louis*'s non-Jewish crew. Women who had been banned from shopping in town markets and department stores now enjoyed the luxuries of the ship's beauty salon. And children not previously allowed to enjoy the parks, playgrounds, and schools of the Reich romped festively together, spending long, happy hours exploring the *St. Louis*'s many nooks and crannies and even indulging in the luxury of the swimming pool. Dance music played every night. Courteous waiters served delicious, multicourse meals.

The man behind the passengers' many comforts was Captain Gustav Schröder, a thirty-seven-year veteran of the Hamburg-America Line. After instructing his 231-member crew that the refugees were paying passengers and must be treated as such, Captain Schröder even took the unprecedented (and politically dangerous) step of removing the ballroom's large formal portrait

of Adolf Hitler, thus better enabling the grand salon to be used as
a place for Jewish worship. "There is a somewhat nervous dispo-
sition among the passengers," the captain wrote in his diary after
the *St. Louis*'s first day at sea. "Despite this, everyone seems convinced they will never see Germany again. Touching departure
scenes have taken place. Many seem light of heart, having left
their homes. Others take it heavily. But beautiful weather, pure
sea air, good food, and attentive service will soon provide the
usual worry-free atmosphere of long sea voyages. Painful im-
pressions on land disappear quickly at sea and soon seem merely
like dreams."[2]

"I just remember running around the ship a lot," recalls Clark
Blatteis, "and generally having a real nice time. It was, after all, a
luxury ship."[3] "I loved it," echoes Sol Messinger, who celebrated
his seventh birthday during the voyage. "I got out from under
my mother's thumb"—something he had not previously been
able to do as a Jewish child growing up amid the dangers of Hitler's Germany. "Oh, we were treated so well," remembers Alice
Oster, a young lady at the time of the voyage. "We walked about.
We heard Strauss music, and we hadn't heard Strauss for a long
time before that."[4]

Despite all the pleasant distractions of the *St. Louis*, Recha
Weiler, aged sixty-one, remained unable to relax. Her husband,
Moritz, a longtime professor from the University of Cologne
who had lost his position after the Nazis came to power, suffered
from congestive heart failure and remained in bed in the couple's
cabin from the moment he first came aboard. For more than a
week, the ship's doctor attended Professor Weiler and prescribed
many different medications. But nothing helped. Finally, on
Tuesday, May 23, Professor Weiler passed away. He was buried
at sea later that same night. Protocol called for the body to be
shrouded in the swastika-emblazoned flag of the Reich; but at his
widow's request, Professor Weiler was draped in the Hamburg-
America ensign.

One wonders how many of the passengers realized the many
dramas Captain Schröder dealt with that Tuesday. Early the
same morning, Schröder had received definitive word that a new
Cuban decree effectively nullified the landing permits held by
most of those aboard the *St. Louis.* He found himself suddenly

confronted with the very real possibility that nearly all of his charges would be denied entry at Havana. "MAJORITY OF YOUR PASSENGERS," cabled the Hamburg-America Line's home office, "IN CONTRAVENTION OF NEW CUBAN LAW 937 AND MAY NOT BE GIVEN PERMISSION TO DISEMBARK. . . . YOU WILL MAINTAIN SPEED AND COURSE, AS SITUATION IS NOT COMPLETELY CLEAR BUT CERTAINLY CRITICAL IF NOT RESOLVED BEFORE YOUR ARRIVAL."[5]

The background to the sudden change in Cuban policy can be sketched briefly. Issued in early 1939, Decree 55 had stated that every immigrant entering Cuba required a $500 bond to guarantee that he or she would not become a burden on the state. But the decree also said tourists and those transiting through Cuba were welcome and did not need visas or to post a bond. Subsequently, Cuba's director of immigration, Manual Benitez Gonzalez, took advantage of this loophole and cashed in by selling "tourist" landing permits for use by people who were in fact refugees. Initially sold and signed by the man commonly known as "Benitez," the landing permits went through several price markups before landing in the hands of German Jews fleeing Hitler.

Captain Schröder had been aware of the possibility of a problem with the landing visas since before leaving Hamburg but had chosen to hope for the best. It had, in fact, been on May 5— eight days before the *St. Louis*'s departure—that Cuban president Frederico Laredo Bru and his cabinet closed the loophole with a new decree. They cited as their rationale Decree 55's potential for exploitation and the fact that the stagnant Cuban economy had no jobs to spare for refugees. In truth, however, the president was also upset over Benitez's actions and was under internal political pressure to turn away the ship.

During midafternoon on May 23, as Recha Weiler prepared to bury her husband in the cold waters of the Atlantic, a five-man committee of passengers impaneled by Schröder to help deal with the impending crisis held their first meeting. Chairman of the committee was Josef Joseph, an attorney who, somewhat ironically, had once been an acquaintance of Joseph Goebbels during the 1920s, before Goebbels became Hitler's chief propagandist.[6] Joseph was traveling on the *St. Louis* with his wife, Lilly, and his thirteen-year-old daughter, Liesl. Other members of the committee included Max Weis, Max Zellner, Arthur Hausdorff, and Herbert Manasse. In the coming days, these gentlemen would play a key role communicating with international relief agencies and advocating on behalf of the passengers.

A bell rang out at four in the morning on Saturday, May 27, to awaken the passengers—few of whom as yet realized there was anything wrong—and signal their arrival in Havana. "I have never jumped out of bed so quickly," one girl wrote in her diary. "The sky is dark blue but I can make out a few white buildings stark against it. There are still stars in the sky. It's like a dream."[7] The ship was not, however, docked at the Hamburg-America pier. Instead, she was anchored in the middle of the harbor. This fact was the subject of bemused but generally unconcerned banter as the passengers sat down for breakfast at half past four. Only later did the *St. Louis*'s distance from the docks begin to seem ominous, after Cuban national police were posted to stand guard at gangways. "The atmosphere quickly became horrible," recalls Herta Fink of Breslau, who traveled on the *St. Louis* as a young mother. "The police of Havana came onto the boat, and they marked an *R* in our passport, which meant 'Return.' The atmosphere was very bad, very bad. But, the captain kept assuring us, you don't have to be afraid; we're not bringing you back to Germany. That's what he kept saying."[8]

Despite Captain Schröder's promises and admonitions, panic broke out among the passengers as well as among relatives waiting for them on shore. A number of these family members chartered small motorboats and, escorted by the Cuban police, came right up to the *St. Louis*. In general, however, family members were not allowed to board, with one exception being the grown son of Recha Weiler who had come from New York to comfort his recently bereaved mother. Additionally, a woman named Hilde Rockow somehow slipped by the police and made her way onto the ship. She found her parents, Siegfried and Margarete Rotholz, and her aunt and uncle, Ernest and Regina Loewenstein, to whom—without even taking the time to give them a hug—she handed $1,700 in cash, departing the ship immediately thereafter so as not to be discovered.

Later that day, twenty-two Jewish passengers holding formal visas, each secured by the posting of the requisite $500 bonds, as well as four Spaniards and two Cuban nationals received

In Havana harbor, friends and relatives of the *St. Louis* passengers attempt to make contact, June 1, 1939. (AP/Wide World)

permission to disembark. The rest, holding the worthless "Benitez Certificates," were told they would have to wait.

"The first Spanish word I learned was *mañana*," recalls Herbert Karliner, who traveled on the *St. Louis* as a twelve-year-old boy. "The Cubans kept saying, 'maybe tomorrow,' but mañana never came."[9] Liesl Joseph Loeb, the daughter of Josef Joseph, remembers the desperation of the passengers. "At the time we were in the harbor of Havana and things just weren't moving along. We had some suicide attempts and there was near panic on board because, as I told you before, many of the men all had had to sign they would never return to Germany and if we had returned to Germany, the only place where we would have ended up was in a concentration camp because we had no homes left. We had no money left and we had nothing left. . . . The world just didn't care."[10]

More than corrupt officials and behind-the-scenes power plays were responsible for the debacle in Havana harbor. Cuba was in the middle of a depression, and her citizens had already been chafing at the large influx of refugees that preceded the *St. Louis* (including some 2,500–4,000 Jews); newcomers were frequently seen as competition for scarce jobs.

Antagonism toward refugees was also the result of a mixture of anti-Semitism and xenophobia. Major Cuban newspapers such as *Diario de La Marina* as well as radio stations and trade unions agitated against immigration and held major rallies in the capital. In fact, the largest anti-Semitic demonstration in Cuban history, organized by a former president and drawing a crowd of forty thousand, had taken place in the capital on May 8, just five days before the *St. Louis* left Germany. Adding to the hostile climate, some Havana as well as provincial newspapers openly fed stereotypes by publishing allegations that Jews were Communists. Fascist influence in Cuba was at its height in the spring of 1939 with right-wing groups like the Cuban Nazi Party actively stirring up anti-immigrant and anti-Semitic sentiments. The timing of the *St. Louis*'s arrival could not have been more unfortunate.

On Sunday, May 28, Lawrence Berenson of the JDC arrived in Cuba from the United States to try to negotiate a way out of the impasse directly with President Bru—a five-day process that led nowhere.[11] Bru made an offer. He said he would admit the passengers if the JDC posted a $453,500 bond ($500 per passenger). Berenson then made a counteroffer, which Bru not only rejected but used as an excuse to break off negotiations entirely on June 2.

The drama as enacted in Havana harbor, meanwhile, reached its tragic crescendo on Tuesday, May 30, when Max Loewe slit his wrists and jumped overboard. Loewe, the recipient of an Iron Cross as a veteran of World War I, walked with a limp, the result of a severe beating at the hands of Nazi guards in Buchenwald. After landing in the waters of the port of Havana, Loewe was rescued by the Cuban police and taken to Calixto Garcia Hospital, where he remained when the *St. Louis* pulled out of the harbor on the morning of June 2.

Passenger committee chairman Josef Joseph described the ship's departure in his diary:

> The sirens signaled the engines and we were moving out of Havana into the sunlit blue Caribbean. To our right we passed the lush colors of tropical gardens, blossoming trees and exciting flora. To the left the docks were bordered by the ostentatiously

ornate buildings of a tropical metropolis. . . . Crowds filled every
space along the shoreline, waving, weeping and watching with
great sadness. Automobiles accompanied us as far as the road-
way permitted. And alongside a motorboat with a gentleman
from the Joint Distribution Committee as well as a HAPAG
[Hamburg-America Line] official who all shouted continuous
encouragement and hopes for a speedy "Wiedersehen," see you
soon. A harbor patrol boat followed them and us. It was their
duty to see that we moved swiftly out of the harbor. But the officer in sight managed to convey his sympathy for our plight. An
indescribable drama of human concern and despair played on
us as we sailed into the twilight of uncertainty. This is one of the
most tragic days on board because we feel cheated for the freedom we had hoped for. What started as a voyage of freedom is
now a voyage of doom.[12]

Instead of returning immediately to Hamburg, Captain Schröder
turned north toward Florida in the hope that the U.S. government would allow the vessel to make a landing. This solution
seemed plausible at first. Both Schröder and his passengers'
committee thought it likely that the United States—home to the
statue that welcomed "huddled masses yearning to breathe
free"—would provide the *St. Louis* wanderers with refuge. After
all, most of the passengers had already completed the paperwork for U.S. visas. "America was a magic word," recalls Liesl
Joseph Loeb. "It was the be-all and end-all. We knew America
would not let us down."[13]

Darkness overtook the *St. Louis* as she approached the Florida
coastline on June 3. The lights of Miami winked in the distance
as beacons of hope. The passengers were close enough to see ho-
tels and automobiles along the beach. To Herbert Karliner, who
peered through binoculars, America looked like an oasis. "The
shoreline was a couple miles away. I'd never seen coconut trees
in my life. I was very impressed." But the view also included a
U.S. Coast Guard boat patrolling American waters. And military
planes shadowed the ship.

"The mood on board was grim," remembers Liesl Joseph
Loeb. "The captain thought maybe he could land the ship at
night, but the shore patrol made sure we kept moving." Herbert
Karliner further recalls: "The children on the ship sent letters to
Mrs. Roosevelt [Eleanor, wife of President Franklin Roosevelt]

but she didn't answer." A cable later went to the president himself: "Most urgently repeat plea for help for the passengers of the *St. Louis*. Mr. President help the nine hundred passengers among them over four hundred women and children." Like his wife, President Roosevelt did not respond. "We all thought," recalls Herta Fink-Hartig, "we all believed that Roosevelt would in the end let us in."[14] But it was not to be. "Remember the garbage barge?" Alice Oster asked recently, referring to the trash-piled vessel that wandered the eastern seaboard of the United States for several months in 1987. "We were the human garbage barge."[15]

All this action played out before the eyes of the American people because the story of the *St. Louis* attracted a great deal of media attention. "Refugee Ship Idles Off Florida Coast," proclaimed the front page of the *New York Times* on June 5. The *Washington Post* echoed with a similar blast: "Coast Guard Trails Tragic Liner as It Wanders Aimlessly in Florida Waters." The people of Miami, the city to which the *St. Louis* passengers came so tantalizingly close, followed the same story on the front page of the *Miami Herald*: "Refugee Vessel Rides at Anchor off Miami Coast—Ship Carrying 908 German Jews Halts for Two Hours while Coast Guard Planes and Ships Patrol Nearby." Edward G. Robinson and other Hollywood stars sent telegrams to President Roosevelt and Secretary of State Cordell Hull in support of the refugees, while editorials in many newspapers condemned man's inhumanity to man (though often stopping short of calling for passengers' entry into the United States).

One might well ask, then, what President Roosevelt could have done when confronted with the *St. Louis* crisis. Quotas established by the 1924 Immigration Act firmly limited by nationality the number of immigrants who could be admitted to the United States during any given year.[16] The German quota for 1939—27,370—had already been reached well before the *St. Louis* set sail.[17] In a best-case scenario Roosevelt could have issued an executive order to admit the passengers on an emergency basis. This action, however, would have had at least three problematic consequences. First, it would have been unfair to the approximately 2,500 Jews who were waiting in Cuba as well as the thousands in Europe who had lower quota numbers than the *St. Louis* passengers who had applied for American visas (the fact that a significant number of passengers had no quota number at all further complicated matters). Second, it would have triggered a huge reaction against the Roosevelt Administration from the powerful anti-immigrant lobby that was reaching the height of its influence just at this time. And finally, it would have encouraged more ships to circumvent immigration policy to gain direct admission to the United States.[18] It was not courageous of Roosevelt to refrain from acting, but given the context of the time and all the constraining factors, some would say it is understandable.

On June 4, A. M. Warren of the State Department's Visa Division formally closed the door on the *St. Louis* passengers with a terse statement: "The German refugees . . . must await their turn [for their formal waiting numbers to come up] before they may be admissible to the United States."[19]

Soon thereafter, on June 7, Captain Schröder reluctantly—and as slowly and circuitously as possible—began heading the ship back to Europe.

On board panic and despair seized passengers. With the *St. Louis* bound for Germany, a mood of desperation permeated the vessel. The refugees organized suicide watch patrols. Jules Wallerstein remembers his father confiding to him that a number of Jewish families would take their lives before the ship arrived at Hamburg. "That to me was a shocker," says Mr. Wallerstein. "I was twelve years old and realized it was the end of my life."[20]

Captain Schröder continued to stall as best he could. He cruised at a very slow rate of speed, thus buying the JDC time in which to arbitrate a solution that would spare the passengers a return to the Reich. At one point Schröder even considered a plan to beach the *St. Louis* off the English coast, set it ablaze, and provoke a rescue. Meanwhile, morale aboard the vessel continued to plummet.

Finally, on June 13, as the ship reached the halfway point on its voyage back to Germany, Morris Troper, Chief of European Operations for the JDC, sent a letter announcing what sounded very much like deliverance. The passengers would disembark in Antwerp, Belgium, and from there be dispersed to four western European countries. France agreed to take in 224 refugees, Belgium 214, the Netherlands 181, and England 287. (Max Loewe, in a Havana hospital, would eventually be shipped to England, bringing the total *St. Louis* émigrés in Britain to 288.) One more

Children attend a birthday party on board the *St. Louis* as it sails back to Europe. (USHMM, gift of Henry Gallant (Heinz Goldstein)

Dr. Josef Joseph, Lilly Joseph, Morris Troper, and Liesl Joseph after the *St. Louis* returned to Antwerp, June 17, 1939. (Museum of Jewish Heritage)

St. Louis passengers prepare to disembark at the port of Antwerp, June 17, 1939.
(Bibliothèque Historique de la Ville de Paris)

individual—Istvan Winkler—was not a refugee but a businessman from Hungary. He returned to his native country after the
St. Louis docked in Antwerp.

After weeks of uncertainty and fear, those aboard the *St.
Louis* now passed into a state of euphoria. Four days later, on

June 17—more than a month after departing Hamburg—the ship arrived at Antwerp. From there the passengers were transported to their allotted countries. While a significant number wound up in the relative safety of Great Britain, the rest found themselves embarking—although they at first might not have realized it—upon yet another perilous journey. In less than a year's time, Germany would control much of Europe, and more than six hundred veterans of the *St. Louis* trapped on the Continent would once again be in the crosshairs of Nazi terror.

3

Kaddish

Inevitably, the start of Sarah's research was dry, mundane, and stark: devising a rough list of those *St. Louis* passengers who perished at the hands of the Nazis.

Of the original 937, one died en route to North America, twenty-eight disembarked legally at Havana, and 287 (later joined by Loewe, to make 288) eventually landed in Great Britain. As for the balance, 620, Sarah guessed that most of these had fallen victim to the Nazis. Indeed, the fact that they were refugees and not native to the countries in which they had been settled only increased that likelihood. Sarah also guessed that of those who were killed, most met their end at Auschwitz, the death camp where the majority of those Jews deported from France, Belgium, and the Netherlands.

It is a cruel irony of Holocaust research that facts concerning the dead are often far more easy to trace, or at least deduce, than is information about the living. Those Jews who survived the Holocaust frequently did so because they managed to stick to the shadows and keep their names *off* rosters and checklists.

This is especially the case with regard to the "Final Solution" imposed on western Europe. In the east, roving extermination units frequently wiped out entire communities in the course of just a few days, with very little paperwork indicating individual names. In the west, however, Nazi functionaries carried out their mission in a much more orderly fashion. There they methodically filled out forms, assembled "deportation lists," and wrote numerous memos. Several reference works by noted Holocaust researcher and Nazi hunter Serge Klarsfeld take the massive

St. Louis passengers on board the *Rhakotis* bound for England arrive in Southampton harbor, June 26, 1939. (USHMM, courtesy of Spaarnestad Fotoarchief)

St. Louis passengers arrive at the Gare du Nord station in Paris, June 1939. (USHMM, courtesy of Bibliothèque Historique de la Ville de Paris)

paper trail left by the bureaucrats of Nazi genocide and use it to document the names of more than one hundred thousand Jews deported from such western European countries as France and Belgium.[1]

For most deportees murdered immediately upon arrival at Auschwitz their mention on the Nazi convoy rosters collected by Klarsfeld constitutes the last acknowledgment of their lives. In the relatively few instances where there is additional paperwork—such as a fragmentary collection of some five thousand Auschwitz prisoner registration cards—this usually signals a prisoner who was spared the gas chamber in order to work in the camp as a forced laborer.

In addition to Klarsfeld's books, other resources at Sarah's disposal included data from the so-called Auschwitz Death Books, a large collection of ledgers chronicling more than seventy-four thousand prisoners who, after being selected as slave laborers, subsequently died of "natural" causes.[2] Also, Sarah possessed figures (recorded by the Nazis) citing how many men, women, and children arrived at Auschwitz in each convoy, the number from each convoy who were immediately gassed, and the number selected for labor.

Given the absence of lists detailing the names of those killed at the camps, Sarah spent a great deal of time over the course of six months triangulating information from various data sets in order to make educated guesses as to the destinies of individuals from the *St. Louis*. After Sarah identified a *St. Louis* passenger on a transport to Auschwitz, she would then check her database of prisoner registrations looking for evidence of possible survival. If a name appeared on a convoy list and then disappeared from all other records, including postwar survivor registries, Sarah was forced to assume that the person in question fell victim to a death sentence shortly after arrival at the camp.

For example, Convoy 19, which left the Drancy transport camp in France for Auschwitz on August 14, 1942, included 1,015 deportees. Among these were five *St. Louis* passengers: Herbert and Vera Ascher, Naftali Begleiter, Arthur Blachmann, and Walter Friedmann. When the convoy arrived in Auschwitz, the Germans selected 115 men to work at the camp; all the others—including women and children—were to be gassed. The Aschers along with Begleiter, Blachmann, and Friedmann disappear from all further records after their placement on the convoy. There are no Auschwitz prisoner registration cards for these prisoners and no listings in the Auschwitz Death Books. Nor have these five deportees turned up in postwar survivor records or testimonies. Thus, absent contradicting information, Sarah marked down all five *St. Louis* passengers on Convoy 19 as missing and presumed dead.

One after another, Sarah ticked off the tragedies. Taking up less than an inch of space in Klarsfeld's work memorializing Jews deported from France, Sarah found Charlotte Skotzki with her husband, Guenther, and their two young daughters, Helge and Inge: all were sent to Auschwitz in the same convoy in 1942. In Klarsfeld's companion volume documenting the transport of Belgium residents, a few sparse lines itemized the Dublon family—Willi and Erna and their little daughters, Lore and Eva, plus Willi's young brother Erich. They were all dispatched, like the Skotzki family, to Auschwitz. (Erich was arrested and transported early on, while Willi, Erna, and the girls successfully evaded the Nazis for several years only to be captured and deported in January 1944.)

Slow, painstaking research brought about more and more discoveries. Over time, numerous slim histories gradually emerged from the sparse data. One of these is the story of the Kaufherr family of three, which was assigned to Belgium after the return of the *St. Louis* but was ultimately separated. Like so many German Jewish men in Belgium at the time of the Nazi attack in May 1940, Joseph Kaufherr was considered an enemy alien and thus a security risk; he was sent to a French refugee camp, where he remained once the Germans overran that country. He was deported to Auschwitz on September 4, 1942. Records show Joseph's daughter, Hannelore, was deported from Belgium to Auschwitz one month before her father. They also reveal that Joseph's wife, Betty Kaufherr, followed her husband and daughter to the same death camp on September 26, 1942. Little else is known about these three passengers' final days.

Still, amid all the sad evidence of entire families sent to their deaths, of young children targeted as much as adults, and of spouses separated forever, Sarah found something surprising. At the end of her review of the Museum's holding, she realized that more than half of the 620 passengers who returned to continental Europe did not appear on any of the main Nazi lists.

Sarah thus had reason to hope that they, and perhaps a few listed deportees—like Rudi Dingfelder of Plauen, Germany, and Benno Joseph of Labiszyn, Poland, both registered as slave laborers— might somehow have managed to survive.

4

Archives, Answers, and Anomalies

Sarah's first research expedition beyond the reference library of the Museum took her, toward the end of 1996, to the New York office of the JDC, the worldwide relief organization that had played such a key role in the *St. Louis* saga.[1] There, sitting at a long table in a cramped room filled with files and documents, Sarah skimmed through several of the many folders marked *St. Louis*. "At most, I hoped to find a few hints about the fate of passengers after they disembarked in Antwerp, but these folders revealed much more." As Sarah soon discovered, the JDC had kept very careful track of the passengers after they returned to Europe. In case after case she found correspondence, records of passengers' ever-changing emigration status, lists showing details of financial support, and manifests of ships booked by the JDC to rescue Jewish refugees, including former *St. Louis* passengers.

Interestingly, JDC files revealed that some passengers had returned to Cuba. Czech-born Arnost and Camilla Roth, together with their twelve-year-old son Harry (originally assigned to France after the return of the *St. Louis*), boarded the SS *San Thome* in Casablanca and sailed to Havana in March 1942. In what must have seemed an eerie coincidence to the Roths, the ship arrived a few days after the Cuban government issued a decree ending further issuance of landing permits for refugees born in Axis countries. Thus the Roths and others who were either German citizens or citizens of German-occupied countries did not clear immigration. But neither were they turned away. Instead, the

Cuban government interned them at Tiscornia—a variation on the American Ellis Island. Later on, after about seven months of effort by JDC officials, the Roths gained their release and settled in Havana. They spent the following nine years in Cuba, where Harry learned to speak Spanish and attended high school and university. The family relocated to the United States in 1951.

In addition to confirming the successful emigration of numerous passengers who wound up in continental Europe, the JDC archive also provided Sarah's first real window into the experiences of those sent to England. Some of these, ironically, were arrested and interned as "enemy aliens" after Germany invaded Poland and Britain declared war on the Axis. Such was the case of husband and wife Selmar and Elsa Biener, both from Magdeburg, who were interned in a camp on the Isle of Mann. Again and again, it seemed, the British government failed to recognize that as Jews these refugees were hardly Nazi sympathizers. To further reduce the threat of espionage, the British even shipped some of the passengers to distant parts of the Commonwealth. Dr. Fritz Kassel of Frankenstein, Germany, spent five years in an internment camp in Victoria, Australia, while Hans Kutner landed at a camp near Montreal.

Three days of research in the JDC archive provided a thick folder of information. Sarah entered the new facts into her database and cross-checked these against information gathered previously— in the process deducing the fates of about ten more passengers, bringing the unaccounted-for list to approximately 350. "We were ready now to share this list with *St. Louis* survivors known to the Museum, hoping they might be able to fill in some details of their own stories as well as provide clues about other survivors. We mailed them the list, together with an explanation of the Museum's project. Then we followed up with phone interviews. It took us from the fall of 1996 until the spring of 1997 to complete the interviews, but it was well worth the time."

Most survivors were glad that the Museum had undertaken research on the *St. Louis.* They saw the project as a memorial to passengers who perished at the hands of the Nazis, and they wanted to share what they knew. During the course of some thirty interviews, Museum staff spoke at the greatest length with one man in particular, Herbert Karliner. A retired baker living near Miami, Karliner was the boy who had learned the word *mañana* while aboard the *St. Louis* in 1939. By 1996, Mr. Karliner was serving as the nominal head of a loosely organized group of former *St. Louis* passengers. This small contingent held a reunion in Miami in May 1989 to commemorate the fiftieth anniversary of the sailing of the ship. With the help of Mr. Karliner and others, Sarah soon had leads on more than forty additional passengers, bringing her unaccounted-for list down to approximately 310. She also harvested a wealth of stories, but few more poignant than that belonging to Mr. Karliner himself.

In April 1999, several years after his first contact with Sarah Ogilvie, Herbert Karliner toured the United States Holocaust Memorial Museum's exhibit on the *St. Louis*. Also visiting the Museum was Sol Messinger, another child of the *St. Louis*. Stopping before a large group photograph taken on the deck of the ship in 1939, Karliner said to Messinger, "Up there is my father, and over there"—he used his finger to point—"is me." The image was of a small boy in short pants and a dress jacket, his arm draped protectively around a pretty little girl, smiling in party clothes. "That was my sister; she died at Auschwitz." His voice was flat, expressionless. "You know what I can't understand?" Karliner said a little later on to Messinger. "We were not allowed in Cuba, and then in 1980, 125,000 Cubans were let into Florida without a question. Some of them were criminals, too. And here we were, nine hundred people running away from Nazis, and we could not come."

Turning to Karliner, Messinger answered, "Herb, I like to think that because of us is why they let them in."[2]

Herbert Karliner was born on September 3, 1926, in Peiskretscham, a town of eighteen thousand in eastern Silesia, close to the German-Polish border. The town included a small but vibrant Jewish community of about one hundred families, all of them anchored by an ornate, centuries-old synagogue located near Peiskretscham's central square. Here Herbert's brother Walter, two years his senior, celebrated his bar mitzvah in 1936. The family also included two girls: Ilse, one year older than Walter, and Ruth, one year younger than Herbert.

Their father Joseph Karliner owned a general store. This business in which he'd been raised was located at the front of a large house he'd inherited from his father. In addition to selling

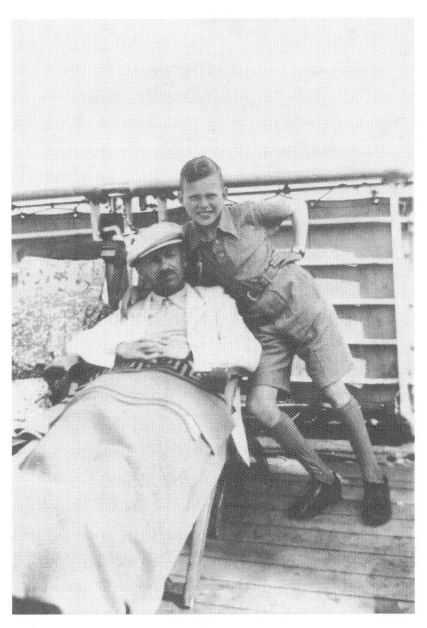

Joseph Karliner and his son Herbert on board the *St. Louis*, May 1939.
(USHMM, courtesy of Herbert Karliner)

groceries and other essentials, Joseph also provided fertilizer to local farmers and in turn bought their grain, which he then sent by freight to city markets. The mother of the family, Martha, was deeply religious and steadfast in her scrupulous adherence to all Jewish religious practices and traditions.

Martha's youngest son, Herbert, remembers the advent of pronounced, Nazi-inspired anti-Semitism in Peiskretscham as something that "simmered slowly" for a long time before finally coming to a boil. "First we were ordered off the sidewalks. Then they banned us from the movie theaters. Eventually my father had to put a sign on the store identifying it as a Jewish business. Also, when I was younger, I liked to play soccer. The teams had both Jewish and Christian players. But as things progressed, I found myself getting kicked around a lot more than the others on the soccer field, and a little afterwards they tossed me off the team altogether. No Jews allowed."[3] Cousins of the Karliners immigrated variously to Palestine and to the United States in the mid-1930s. "But my parents hesitated," remembers Mr. Karliner. "They kept hoping things would get better."

The watershed moment for the Karliners—as for so many other German Jews—was Kristallnacht. "We slept in the house right behind the store, yet we heard nothing," Mr. Karliner says. "Still, in the morning we found the place ransacked. My father was stunned, and just as he and we stood there staring at the mess that had been our business, neighbors came running and said the synagogue was on fire. So we went there. We saw the building ablaze, and we watched the SS with their torches making a bonfire of the prayer books and the Torah. My father tried to save the Torah, but the Nazis beat him up."

Making the rounds of Jewish homes later that day, the SS picked up Joseph Karliner and placed him under arrest. (They did the same with virtually every other Jewish head of household in Peiskretscham.) "We did not see him for three weeks," remembers Mr. Karliner, whose mother had to promise the family's departure from Germany within six months in order to gain her husband's freedom. "They kept him at Buchenwald. When he came home, he was unrecognizable. His head had been shaved, and he'd lost a great deal of weight. But he refused to talk about it. He refused to say a word." (Several weeks after his father's return, young Herbert visited an aunt in a nearby village. The

aunt's husband had been taken to Dachau following Kristallnacht and had yet to return. Herbert was chatting with his aunt,
enjoying a cookie, when a knock came on the door, which
opened to reveal a tall SS man holding a little box—almost like a
pastry box—tied up with string. "Here," the SS man said gruffly
to Karliner's aunt, pushing the box into her hands, "here is your
husband.")

The Karliners' store did not reopen after Kristallnacht. The
parents instead focused their energies on planning the family's
exodus from the Reich. Thus, with time ticking away, they came
to be on board the *St. Louis* in May 1939. "We sold the house and
the business," Mr. Karliner recalls. "The Gestapo came, did an
appraisal, and dictated the price, which was about one-third of
fair value. Also, my parents were made to pay double-duty on
everything we took out of Germany: jewelry, clothes, and other
such things."

Upon the *St. Louis*'s return to Europe, the JDC assigned the
Karliners to France. Disembarking a transport ship at Boulogne,
older sister Ilse went with her parents to live near Poitiers under
the sponsorship of the JDC, while the three younger children
journeyed to the Villa Helvitia children's home near Paris run by
the Oeuvre de Secours aux Enfants (Agency for the Rescue of
Children), popularly known as the OSE. After the outbreak of the
war in September, the children were removed to the Château de
Chaûmont home in central France. "Here we stayed for a number of months," Mr. Karliner remembers. "Me and thirteen or
fourteen other kids celebrated our bar mitzvahs at the school. I
remember the mayor of the town was a Jewish woman, and she
brought a present for each youngster on the big bar mitzvah day.
We, the boys, were all learning carpentry at the time. So each of
us got a tool of some kind, and we were meant to share. Not long
after that my parents came to visit and took Ruth back to Poitiers
with them." This seemingly innocent move, resulting from a
combination of homesickness on Ruth's part as well as her parents' feeling that Ruth would not be comfortable in the Chaûmont home, would have dire consequences later on.

During the autumn of 1940, after the German defeat of
France, the OSE moved their charges from the Château de Chaûmont home to several old castles in the south of the country, as
far away as possible from oncoming German forces. During

this move, Herbert and Walter were separated. Though they would not see each other again until after the end of the war, they remained in sporadic touch through letters. Meanwhile, the fourteen-year-old Herbert was assigned by the OSE to take up a position with a baker some three kilometers away from the castle where he lived. "I walked there and back, morning and night, and spent twelve hours at the place every day apprenticing under an old man whose son had been drafted into the French army. He treated me very nice and taught me many things. I worked for him for two years with only one break, in 1941, when I took some time off and went, illegally, to visit my parents and sisters at Poitiers."

Mr. Karliner vividly remembers his journey, without papers, from the so-called "Free Zone" to the German "Occupied Zone." The fifteen-year-old walked some thirty kilometers, sleeping several nights in haystacks along the way, before arriving at his mother and father's small apartment. "My mother had a job of some kind, but my father was not allowed to work. Also my older sister had work as a secretary somewhere. So my younger sister and my father stayed home and kept house. I stayed about two weeks and was sad to go." It was the last time he would see any of them.

Young Karliner's life continued uninterrupted for nearly another year, until August 26, 1942, when Vichy French police began rounding up children from OSE schools in the Free Zone. The Vichy authorities took Herb to a camp but soon released him and all other children under sixteen. (Those sixteen and over, meanwhile, went to the Drancy transit camp, not far from Paris, and from there to Auschwitz.) "I was very lucky," Mr. Karliner remembers. "I was just days short of my sixteenth birthday. They let me go, and I spent the next three years under the protection of the OSE in its various guises. I had false papers showing my name as 'Paul Braun' and indicating my birthplace as Alsace-Lorraine, the latter chosen because I was so clearly German."

For a time he was part of an OSE party endeavoring to get to Palestine via southern France and Spain. When that venture failed, he lived on an OSE-sponsored farm in Lyon. "I was in touch with my parents, on and off, until the early autumn of '42. But on the sixth of November I received a card from another couple in Poitiers, friends of my sister Ilse, saying the family had been arrested. After that I had only a few letters from my sickly father, who'd been separated from my mother and sisters and confined to the Rothschild Hospital in Paris. Then eventually, after January of 1944, I had no further word from him either."

By the spring of 1944, Herbert, still posing as Paul Braun, had found employment as a hired hand assisting a pro-Vichy farmer who thought him a Catholic. The farm was about twenty kilometers from Lyon. "I went to mass every Sunday," he recalls. "I had to be careful, because I was now of fighting age and the Germans, desperate for men, were drafting everyone in sight, including Frenchmen, which I supposedly was." Herbert eventually left the farm and went into hiding several months before the Americans took Lyon in September 1944. "I only came out of the woods when I saw the American tanks. I told them I wanted to join up with them, which of course was impossible. Eventually I reconnected, for the last time, with the OSE, and they shipped me to Paris for the duration."

After the close of the war, Herbert reunited with his brother Walter (who, much like Herbert, had lived out the war in the protection of the OSE, under an assumed name, working on farms). They met, per a previously arranged family plan, at Poitiers, there to wait several weeks before coming to the grim realization that their mother, father, and sisters were no more. Information from the Red Cross soon confirmed a few details: around September 1942, German authorities dispatched Martha Karliner and her daughters to Drancy and then to Auschwitz, where they were killed. Joseph Karliner, meanwhile, who had been ill and a patient at the Rothschild Hospital in Paris, was deported to Auschwitz on November 20, 1943.

Sponsored by relatives, Herbert and Walter left France and came, at long last, to the United States in 1947. "When I saw Miami Beach [from the decks of the *St. Louis*]," recalls Mr. Karliner, "I said to myself: 'I have to come back.'"[4] He opened a bakery and made use of the skills he had learned as an apprentice in wartime France. But before he embarked on his career, he served in the U.S. Army, fighting in Korea. "Uncle Sam didn't want me in 1939," he says somewhat ruefully. "But he sure wanted me in 1950!"

During March 1997, not long after her visit to the JDC's New York headquarters, Sarah had the opportunity to attend a meeting at Israel's national Holocaust memorial and documentation center, Yad Vashem in Jerusalem. Sitting before a microfilm reader in Yad Vashem's large research library, Sarah scrolled through the records of the Red Cross International Tracing Service (ITS), an organization established after the war to help Holocaust survivors find their missing relatives. (On the day Sarah visited, she was joined by more than a dozen survivors from around the world. Several were quite old and frail, all still seeking lost loved ones some fifty years after World War II.)

Sarah systematically made her way through the names of unaccounted-for *St. Louis* passengers. By the end of the day, she had found data on several dozen, many of whom had survived the war by going into hiding. A few, however, did not fit this simple algorithm. Take, for example, Samuel Weisz and Mauritius Stein. Completely contrary to the pattern of most Jews in western Europe, who usually did their best to move away from Nazi power, Samuel and Mauritius actually abandoned Britain, where they had been assigned after the *St. Louis*'s return, and journeyed east to their native Romania, where some 50 percent of the Jewish population would eventually be killed. Nevertheless, according to ITS data, Samuel and Mauritius did survive, perhaps because they settled in the city of Bucharest where, despite what was happening elsewhere in Romania and throughout the rest of Europe, most Jews were spared extermination.[5]

After learning the fate of Samuel and Mauritius, Sarah was left with much work to do and only about an hour before the archive closed. "I began to check the names of passengers I already knew had been deported but for whom we had no definitive death date. I went down the list alphabetically, looking for the Aschers, the Bendheims, the Camnitzers, and so on." As Sarah had suspected would be the case, family after family appeared to have vanished without a trace. "When I reached the letter D, the pattern appeared to be the same. Johanna and Leopold Dingfelder were arrested in Holland, interned in the Westerbork transit camp, and deported to Auschwitz. Nothing indicated they had survived the initial SS selection of prisoners. At ages fifty-two and fifty-seven, respectively, they most likely had been gassed immediately."

However, information concerning their son Rudi suggested a completely different chain of events. Sarah had previously found an Auschwitz prisoner registration for Rudi Dingfelder, who, though arrested at the same time as his parents, had remained in the Netherlands a full year before being shipped to Auschwitz. There, as the prisoner registration made clear, the nineteen-year-old survived initial selection and worked as part of the forced labor pool. But now, in the Red Cross ITS records, Sarah found even more detail on Rudi's wartime experience. It appeared that after Auschwitz he'd worked at several forced-labor sites within Germany. In fact, according to the ITS data, Dingfelder's last known location was Schwerin, Germany, his place of incarceration during February 1945. The ITS files had nothing to reveal about what happened next to Rudi. Nevertheless, given his youth and the fact that he was clearly still alive just three months before V-E Day, it seemed tantalizingly likely to Sarah that Rudi Dingfelder might possibly be the first death camp survivor identified among the hundreds of *St. Louis* deportees. (Concerning Sarah's one other *St. Louis* passenger registered as an Auschwitz prisoner, Benno Joseph of Poland, the ITS records remained silent.) Some measure of hope, at least, seemed reasonable.

Upon her return to Washington later that month, Sarah could say with all honesty that she had conducted a credible review of available documentation regarding Holocaust victims. But she could likewise express her genuine surprise that more than half of the 620 passengers left stranded on mainland Europe had not turned up on arrest, deportation, or wartime internment lists. "This," says Sarah, "suggested a conclusion that was hard to absorb at first, so counter was it to our starting assumption. Could it actually be that the passengers we had yet to find were *survivors?*"

If this were true, Sarah would not have to travel far to test the hypothesis. Since most *St. Louis* passengers had been trying since 1939 (and before) to get to the United States, it stood to reason that at least some survivors would have wound up coming to the U.S. after the war. And the National Archives, with its rich bounty of immigration and census records, was just on the other side of the National Mall.

"I convinced a reluctant intern from Germany, who did not believe the survival hypothesis, to go over there and check a few names," Sarah remembers. "And I asked him to be sure to look for Rudi Dingfelder, because I quite simply hadn't been able to stop thinking about Rudi since following his ITS trail to its end in February 1945." Hours later, Sarah was sitting in her office when the intern came running through the door. "He survived! Rudi Dingfelder is a survivor! And he's not the only one!" the intern shouted, handing over a folder containing photocopies listing more than a dozen immigrants whose names and vital statistics matched those of *St. Louis* passengers.

Sarah studied the paperwork for Rudi Dingfelder. "Even though I had a hunch it might happen, I was still astounded to see this document that confirmed his arrival in the United States two years after the war. He even had a brother in this country at the time, in Michigan." But a subsequent search of telephone directories and various public records failed to shed any further light on Rudi, who seemed to have vanished the moment he landed in the United States.

Nevertheless, after that successful day, Sarah and several Registry colleagues made repeated visits to the reading room at the National Archives in search of other *St. Louis* passengers who might have eventually found their way to the American mainland. They sat at microfilm readers for hours, combed ships' manifests, and tried alternative spellings whenever they were at first unsuccessful in finding a passenger's name. "Sometimes a name that seemed to match a passenger's would appear in the main index, but when we checked the actual manifest, it would be illegible," Sarah remembers. "Other times the roll of microfilm itself was missing. In those cases we were left with promising hints but no actual confirmation that a passenger survived. Some days, after we had spent hours poring over tiny print in the dark, stuffy reading room, we would return to the Museum with no new information. The more time that passed, the further apart our successes became." Still, the exercise at the National Archives enabled Sarah to get down to one hundred the names remaining on her unaccounted-for list. "In the end, we realized that we had exhausted what the National Archives could tell us. We needed a new strategy, a new approach."

5

The First Israeli Survivor

The new approach Sarah needed came in the form of new
blood: a recent recruit to the Survivors' Registry by the
name of Scott Miller. Scott had been employed by the Museum
since 1989, first as a research historian for the multimedia Wexner Learning Center and later as the academic programs coordi-
nator for the Research Institute. Unlike Sarah, Scott was Jewish.
He also spoke fluent Hebrew, could read and write Yiddish, and
had spent considerable time in Israel. Raised in the Bronx, just
north of New York's Washington Heights, Scott graduated from
Columbia University in 1980 with a degree in history; he then
earned an MA from the Jewish Theological Seminary. He had
also done work toward a doctorate in Jewish history at the Hebrew University in Jerusalem. First visiting Israel in 1978, Scott
subsequently worked on a kibbutz in the Negev desert. Through
much of 1980 and 1981 he taught English in a high school in the
Galilee, and from 1983 to 1988 he taught classes in Jewish history
at a variety of Israeli schools for American students while pursu-
ing his studies at the Hebrew University.

> I moved to Israel because I grew up belonging to a Zionist youth
> organization and attending Jewish summer camps. Thus I am a
> believer in the national, cultural, and political revival of the Jew-
> ish people in their own land. I had, and still have, many friends
> from childhood who settled in Israel, all of whom believe in
> what we call "fulfillment through aliyah." I still go back to Israel
> quite often. And, you know, I think about the *St. Louis* passen-
> gers every time I land at Ben Gurion Airport and go through cus-
> toms. How very inspiring it is that now there is a country where

Jews control the ports of entry: one place in the world where an immigration official will never say there are "too many Jews in this country."[1]

Like Sarah, Scott never planned on working in a Holocaust-related field and surprised himself when he wound up taking a position with the United States Holocaust Memorial Museum.

> Growing up in a Jewish neighborhood I always knew about the Holocaust, of course, but it was not spoken about nearly as much as today. The issues of concern when I was a kid were the Jewish issues of the day: freedom of immigration for Soviet Jews, the Six Day War, etc. The Holocaust was simply the model of what could happen if things went wrong again, but we didn't delve into it. I have always known about the *St. Louis* though. When I was in high school and college I remember the first books coming out about American apathy and the Holocaust. Morse's book, *While Six Million Died,* was the first. He had a whole chapter on the *St. Louis* which I remember reading in college and being captivated by.

Nevertheless, Scott was not enthusiastic when Sarah first recruited him to help with her research.

> I literally thought she was nuts. I believed most of the *St. Louis* passengers perished. It was supposedly "common knowledge." So what, I thought, was the point of trying to determine their fates in detail? Also, I believed that even *if* the fates of the passengers were more varied and nuanced than previously thought, it would be impossible to find out—after all these years—what happened. I did not think the records or the personal testimony would be available. And personally I was most interested in the broader lessons of the Holocaust rather than focusing on individual stories. In fact, I believed that researching personal stories was an unseemly exercise of macabre voyeurism. Now, of course, I realize that revealing the fates and telling the tales of individuals who died in the Holocaust is paying them a posthumous honor, but earlier I believed that exposing individual stories was something like trampling on the dead, walking on graves, intruding on the privacy of the dead.

What was more, much of the detail work associated with Sarah's quest—tedious hours spent combing through endless lists of the living and dead—did not interest Scott. Thus he hesitated to get involved for several months before a list from Herbert Karliner itemizing *St. Louis* survivors who had attended the fiftieth anniversary event in Florida caught his eye and piqued his interest. Scott noticed that every one of Mr. Karliner's alumni was based in the United States. Surely, he thought, there had to be at least some *St. Louis* passengers who eventually wound up in Israel. But how to trace them? How to begin the quest?

It was a friend at the *Jerusalem Post* who told Scott his best bet for reaching German-speaking Israelis would be Israel's leading German-language newspaper, *Israel Nachtrichten*. Subsequently, Scott arranged for that paper to publish an account of the Museum's search for *St. Louis* survivors together with a list of unaccounted-for passengers. The announcement appeared in the April 3, 1997, edition.

Among the unaccounted-for passengers being sought at that point was a family of three, Manfred and Herta Fink and their little boy, Michael. The initial records gathered by Sarah showed that the Finks were sent from Rotterdam to Westerbork and then to Theresienstadt, at which point the paper trail of evidence stopped. Thus the fate of the Finks remained a mystery up until the morning of April 3, when a man in the Tel Aviv suburb of Ramat HaSharon received a telephone call from his mother-in-law, herself a survivor and a reader of *Israel Nachtrichten*. "Michael," the woman said, "they are looking for you in Washington."

Later that same morning, Scott Miller opened up an e-mail on his computer. "My name is Michael Barak," read the note's opening line, "but in 1939 on board the *St. Louis* it was Michael Fink. I was four years old the day we harbored in Antwerp. My father, Manfred Fink, my mother Herta, and I were sent to Westerbork and spent the main part of the Second World War there until 1944 when we were deported to Theresienstadt. My father was sent promptly to Auschwitz and died in transit of some disease. My mother and I survived, were sent back to Holland from where we came to Palestine, now the State of Israel. My mother died six months ago at the age of eighty-six."[2]

In a phone conversation later that same day, Michael Barak told Scott that the Holocaust Museum had been looking for the right person but for the wrong name. Many years earlier Michael

Manfred, Michael, and Herta Fink in the Westerbork internment camp during World War II. (USHMM, courtesy of Michael Barak)

changed the family name from Fink to Barak. He applauded the Museum's *St. Louis* research, but he also added bitterly, "Mr. Miller, I hold the United States responsible for the death of my father. My father, like the other nine hundred passengers on the *St. Louis,* was off the coast of Miami, and he ended up at Auschwitz. How did that happen, Mr. Miller?"[3]

Eventually, Scott and Sarah were able to visit Mr. Barak at his home, where several hours of talk yielded the details of his story. Mr. Barak could not remember much about the actual voyage of the *St. Louis.* However, his memories of the events that followed the ship's fateful return to Europe were quite vivid. He recalled, for example, living in Rotterdam in a small hotel. And he shared the contents of various letters his father, Manfred, had sent to his brother Heinz in New York City. One note dated July 28, 1939, read in part:

We expressed interest in traveling to Chile; the visa along with a work permit costs $250 and we would be obligated to work for one year in a construction area. But where would we get the dollars, and the passage can only be booked at the beginning of 1940. The travel costs would be paid by the [Joint Distribution] Committee here. So we have to simply wait for it . . . Everybody here is now or later going to the USA. I haven't registered with the American consulate since that costs one dollar and I have no money, but I want to try to get the money from the local committee. We must report the names of our relatives since the people from the committee want to know who here will pay for our living costs. If I can get a good affidavit, I would like to register here [Rotterdam] at the consulate. Affidavits are very complicated, and need to include details of monthly income, complete documentation, and a declaration that the person giving the affidavit will provide monthly income for the subject to live on; otherwise the local consul will not acknowledge it. . . . [British-controlled] Palestine has been closed [to immigration] for six months and therefore is not a possibility. There is no possibility of traveling any farther.[4]

Four months later, Mr. Fink wrote once again to his brother Heinz. "We want and hope that Holland can stay neutral. If I could go to the construction site in Chile and have to do hard labor there, I would go there immediately because you have absolutely no possibilities here and you are always in the middle of the European witches' kettle."[5]

Germany invaded the Netherlands on May 10, 1940. Four days later the Dutch police rounded up the Finks—who were considered German interlopers and potential fifth columnists—and placed them in the Westerbork internment camp. "We were behind barbed-wire fences," remembered Michael. "We were placed behind barbed wire not because we were Jews, but because we were Germans."

The Netherlands capitulated on May 15. At first, the new German administration did not pose an immediate threat to the Finks or other internees at Westerbork. Dutch authorities continued to administer the camp into 1942, and life proceeded in a deceptively routine manner. Michael attended school. The camp even included a synagogue. When young Michael became ill, Dutch doctors treated him and brought him back to health. People sent and received mail. The Finks regularly exchanged letters with relatives in the United States, but no word came from loved ones—among them Michael's four grandparents—in Germany.[6]

Barak remembered it was in mid-1943 when he first saw people in Westerbork being forcibly loaded onto trains. This scene repeated itself with increasing frequency throughout the coming months. Finally, on September 9, 1944, came the Finks' turn. Approaching nine years of age, Michael had no idea of their destination or why they were being sent away. He slept through most of the ride, and the next day he awoke in the Theresienstadt ghetto near Prague.

The story of Theresienstadt is complex and intriguing. Established by the Germans for propaganda purposes as a "model" ghetto, Theresienstadt at the time the Finks arrived (a few months after a Red Cross inspection team) boasted dormitories, a library with some sixty thousand volumes, and an active cultural life. Having gathered a large number of Jewish intellectuals and artists at the camp, the Germans even went so far—for a while—as to allow choirs, orchestras, operas, theater troupes, and cabarets. The ghetto had been "beautified" for the Red Cross visit and all these elements loomed large when the officials came to call, just as did the smiling children kicking balls across fields and elders playing cards.

Immediately after the Finks' arrival at Theresienstadt the place still seemed habitable. Dormitory conditions were better than what the family had left behind in the Netherlands. Michael made many friends. In fact, as he told Sarah and Scott, he "played" his way "through the early days at Theresienstadt." Music filled the air and food was available. The Finks did not yet realize that Theresienstadt doubled as a transit station on the road to Auschwitz. Death camp deportations had been stepped up immediately before the Red Cross inspection so as to ease any sense of overcrowding, and they would soon be stepped up again. (Of the 140,000 Jews sent to Theresienstadt between 1941 and 1945, nearly ninety thousand of them would eventually be deported to points east and almost-certain death.)

The Finks were not long at Theresienstadt when conditions began to deteriorate. Trains came and went at a steadily increasing rate carrying human cargo in and out. In time, the Germans deported the ghetto's leadership and most of the artists and musicians. The choirs and orchestras stopped. Through the fall and winter of 1944, food grew increasingly scarce. Children with whom Michael had played one day would, the next morning, be suddenly absent. Others—including Michael's father, infected with typhus—vanished just as mysteriously. For reasons he still does not understand, Michael did not immediately ask his mother about his father's whereabouts. "Who asked questions?" But when he finally did raise the subject, Herta told him his father had died on a train en route to Auschwitz. She likewise told him, eventually, that all four of his grandparents had been murdered by the Nazis.

Against the odds, Michael and his mother never found themselves on a convoy to death. During the spring of 1945, their German guards began to desert and retreat. Then finally, on May 8, nearly five years to the day after their first incarceration by the Dutch, liberating Soviet soldiers approached the camp on horseback. Soon thereafter the Russians ordered Herta and Michael to pack their clothes and board an open truck along with ten to fifteen other people. Michael sat on suitcases. Transported to the Czech border, Michael and his mother were there received by American soldiers, who eventually brought them back to Amsterdam, where they moved into an apartment with friends from their days at Westerbork.

Later that same month, Michael's mother enrolled him in a Zionist youth house near the town of Dieren. The couple who ran the home instilled in Michael and his nine classmates the teachings of pioneering Zionism. The children also attended religious services and read from the Torah. It was here that Michael first studied the basic tenets of Judaism. Although he had been targeted and persecuted for years because of his Jewish heritage, it was only after the Holocaust that he began to truly understand and relate to his Jewish identity.

In mid-1946, veterans of the "Jewish Brigade" visited the home in Dieren. The only independent, national Jewish military formation to serve with the Allies during World War II (a unit of the British Colonial Forces), the Jewish Brigade was comprised mainly of settlers from Eretz Israel. Numbering some five thousand troops, these Jewish infantry, artillery, and service units trained in Egypt and then, in 1944, took part in the final battles of the war on the Italian front. During May 1945, as European hostilities ceased, the brigade moved to northeast Italy and encountered Holocaust survivors for the first time. Finally, in the summer of 1946, after more than a year of various missions of occupation, the Jewish Brigade disbanded. It was at this point that various veterans of the outfit began touring displaced-persons camps and schools— such as the school in Dieren. The veterans sought to educate Holocaust survivors about Zionism, to recruit candidates for immigration to Palestine, and to facilitate that immigration.

With his mother's encouragement and carrying a valid British visa, Michael traveled to Palestine accompanied by brigade veterans in late 1946. He was ten years old. From Dieren, the vets took Michael and other children on trains to the ship *Cairo* in Marseille, France. Then the *Cairo* carried them to Palestine, where young Michael was at first not treated very well by his fellow classmates at the Tel Ra'anan religious school in B'nei B'rak. Ironically, the sabra (Israeli-born Jews) related to Holocaust survivors with scorn. "Why hadn't the Jews of Europe stood up for themselves?" they asked. Michael had no response.

Herta moved to Palestine one month before the 1948 War of Independence. She would spend the rest of her life there, although Michael says today that she was not a true Zionist and that Israel was never really her home. She wanted to start a new life away from Europe, but she could have lived that life anywhere. Milwaukee, Tokyo, Haifa—it made no difference to her, save that her son was in Israel. Herta refused to learn Hebrew. Eventually she settled in Ramat Gan where she worked as a cleaning lady and married another German Jew in the early 1950s.

During mid-1953, just as Michael was about to enter the Israeli army, he had his surname legally changed from Fink to Barak. Recalling a great Jewish warrior from the Book of Judges, the name Barak denotes the Zionist ideals of bravery, physical prowess, and self-reliance.

Michael Barak met his future wife, Ruth—the daughter of Holocaust survivors—in 1960. Today the couple have three grown children. Their eldest son, Roey, is a distinguished colonel in the Israeli army. More than sixty years after the voyage of the *St. Louis*, refugee Michael Fink Barak has succeeded in forging a new Zionist identity for himself and his family.

Several months after Sarah and Scott interviewed Michael Barak at his home, additional archival records telling a different story surfaced concerning his father, Manfred Fink.

Although infected with typhus, Manfred must have been healthy enough—or at least he must have appeared healthy enough—to survive the first-round selection on his arrival at Auschwitz. One month later, in October 1944, he was transported from the main Auschwitz death camp to the SS-managed quarry and cement factory at Golleschau. After Golleschau the Nazis moved him to the Sachsenhausen concentration camp near Berlin. Then, in February 1945, they transferred him yet again, putting him on a train to the Flossenbürg concentration camp, a ramshackle collection of frigid dormitories hugging the rim of a granite quarry in Bavaria, near the Czech border.

On March 8, less than a month after his arrival at Flossenbürg and less than two months before the liberation of that camp, the Nazis moved Fink one last time—to Bergen-Belsen, where his paper trail ends. It must be assumed that Manfred Fink perished there. Located north of Hanover near the city of Celle, Bergen-Belsen had once been in use as a prisoner-of-war camp but by 1944 served as a dumping ground for prisoners evacuated from the outskirts of the rapidly shrinking Third Reich. During the early months of 1945, sick and starving survivors of death marches from the east were forced into the camp. When British troops liberated Bergen-Belsen on April 15, 1945, they found thousands of unburied corpses and approximately sixty thousand survivors, most of whom were very ill. Of these, nearly half were to die in the weeks following liberation. During the same month that Manfred Fink arrived at Bergen-Belsen, Anne Frank and her sister Margot, inmates of the same camp, met their end.

Confronted with the new archival information about his father's last days, Michael Barak quickly thought of an explanation as to the difference between what the records showed and the information Herta had repeated through the years. "A man who was on the train with my father [came back later and] claimed that my father died on the train from Theresienstadt. I must thank my good fortune that my mother, who never knew about those facts, died before I had to tell her this."

The discovery of Michael Barak and his story reduced Sarah and Scott's unaccounted-for list by three, leaving the balance at ninety-seven.

6

A Total American

Saturday, Labor Day Weekend, 1998: Bert Blackburn listened with half an ear to National Public Radio's *Weekend Edition* while driving around El Paso, Texas. NPR's lead story for the day sounded vaguely familiar. It was about that ship—*What was she called again?*—full of Jewish refugees sent back to Europe by Franklin Roosevelt. Terrible story. Blackburn remembered the movie, *Voyage of the Damned.* Terrible movie. It needed a better screenwriter and a better director. Maybe Martin Scorsese. Perhaps someday if Scorsese directed a remake Blackburn would go see it.

Weekend Edition host Scott Simon spent a good twenty minutes lobbing questions at guests Sarah Ogilvie and Scott Miller. After sketching the overall tale of the *St. Louis,* the two researchers went on to describe their particular focus at that moment: one Rudi Dingfelder. Originally from Plauen, Germany, Rudi had traveled on the *St. Louis* as a fifteen-year-old with his parents and wound up in the Netherlands after the ship's return to Europe. A gifted fledgling engineer, Rudi—unlike his father and mother, Leopold and Johanna—survived the war as a slave laborer for the Germans. Furthermore, recent research at the National Archives had revealed the 1947 emigration from the Netherlands of a Rudi Dingfelder who appeared to be one and the same.

Nevertheless, as Sarah and Scott told Scott Simon during the interview, they remained at an impasse with regard to this particular *St. Louis* "survivor." No telephone listings or other pertinent records could be found for anyone named Rudi Dingfelder

Leopold, Johanna, and Rudi Dingfelder on board the *St. Louis*, May/June 1939. (USHMM, courtesy of Gerri Felder)

anywhere in the United States anytime after 1947. Perhaps some-one listening could provide a lead. Sarah and Scott hoped so. In the end, however, it was Scott Simon's voice-over conclusion that finally got Dr. Blackburn's unequivocal attention. "This man is believed to have settled in Michigan, where he worked as a tool-maker, joining a brother who had already emigrated in the 1930s. Rudi Dingfelder would be about seventy-four today."[1]

Dr. Blackburn knew of a distant relative, now deceased—the father of his wife's sister-in-law—who fit the description of Rudi Dingfelder. Bob Felder was a German Jew and an Auschwitz sur-vivor who had lost both parents in the Holocaust. He had arrived in America from the Netherlands in 1947, joining a brother who lived in Michigan. Plus he had been a toolmaker as a young man. His name, however, was quite obviously different. And Black-burn had never heard of any association with the *St. Louis*. Later, after Blackburn's wife came home and he informed her of the radio report, she called her sister-in-law, Joanne Bass of West Bloomfield, Michigan, who confirmed that her father, Bob Felder, was indeed Rudi Dingfelder of the *St. Louis*. Joanne subsequently agreed to be put in touch with the Museum researchers.

In the spring of 2001, Gerri Felder, widow of Bob Felder, who died in 1986 at the age of sixty-two, sat with Museum staff members in the dining room of her Michigan home. She spoke haltingly and with a slight accent. Gerri was born in Germany to a Jewish father and Christian mother, and like her husband, spent time in the Netherlands after growing up in Germany.

> Bob would not have enjoyed this publicity. He never made a big "to-do" about the past. He didn't like to talk about it, and he didn't think his experiences made him special. He said lots of people went through what he did. I remember when we went to Israel in 1981 and the bus stopped at Yad Vashem. I did not want to go inside, and I asked Bob, "Are you going in to see?" He said, "No. Why should I? I lived what they talk about in there. They have nothing to tell me about the Holocaust." So we both skipped it; but before we left Israel we planted a tree for his parents. Besides that, the only time I ever saw him get sentimental about such things—and this happened every year—was at Yom Kippur when he would say Kaddish for his mother and father. He always broke down, always. But otherwise he was a very strong man who preferred to look forward rather than back, and who was committed to his new life in this new world. He never went to be interviewed for his story like so many other survivors. Still, he did not try to blot out his story either. When an idiot told him once that the Holocaust never happened, Bob rolled up his sleeve and showed him the numbers: his tattoo from Auschwitz. "You're right," he said. "There was no such thing as the Holocaust. See these numbers? I did it myself because it looks so pretty." He loved his mother very much, and he respected his father, who was very strict.[2]

In the days before the rise of the Nazis, the Dingfelder family owned a prosperous butcher shop in Germany. But all this was gone by 1939, when Rudi—then a promising young student with a knack for machines and math—embarked on the *St. Louis* with his parents, hoping to eventually get to the United States where Rudi's older brother was already living. "His brother Martin had sized things up and got out of there." In fact Rudi's brother had come to the United States in 1938 at the age of seventeen. At the time of the journey of the *St. Louis*, he was staying in Cleveland with his uncle Carl, the brother of the older Mr. Dingfelder, who likewise was the sponsor for Rudi and his parents on their applications for American visas.

The Dingfelder family butcher shop, Plauen,
Germany, c. 1925. (USHMM, courtesy of Gerri
Felder)

Long after they had made contact with Gerri Felder, Sarah
and Scott discovered that Carl had traveled to England from the
United States when the *St. Louis* was forced to return to Europe,
hoping he could be of help to his brother and family. Museum
staff found a napkin in a collection donated by the daughter of
Morris Troper, the Chief of European Operations for the JDC
who helped broker the arrangement that allowed the passengers
to avoid returning to Germany. The napkin contained a plea
scrawled by Leopold Dingfelder for his family to be allowed to
go to England to join Carl, a request that was not to be fulfilled.

The Dingfelders were instead assigned to the Netherlands
where at first they led a comfortable existence in the town of
Gouda. Even after the German invasion in 1940, life continued
to be relatively normal for a while, and Rudi earned good wages
as a toolmaker. All this changed, however, when Rudi and his
parents were arrested by the Gestapo on October 12, 1942.

Within months, after only a short time at the Westerbork transit camp, the SS put Rudi's parents on a transport to Auschwitz. Rudi, meanwhile, remained behind in the Netherlands, where he worked at the Dornier aircraft factory as a slave laborer. There he stayed until March 1944 when he was deported to Auschwitz. Upon his arrival at Auschwitz, as prisoners were being dragged off the train by camp guards, Rudi panicked as he lost his glasses. Of approximately 2,500 people in Rudi's convoy, only fifty-five survived initial selection. During the selection process, Rudi noticed that nearly all the people wearing glasses were sent to the line for death. Thus he counted his blessings for what seemed at first to be bad luck.

In a letter written in broken English shortly after his liberation in 1945, Rudi described how those spared the gas chamber had to work very hard while receiving little food, inspired only by the threat of beatings or worse. "This life I did hold out for six days," he wrote, "then I break down. Fortunately, the same day a few engineers of the Siemens-Schuckert factories came to the camp. They were looking for special instrument makers. I was examined three times and then engaged by the firm; and I went to work at the Bobreck Siemens camp [an Auschwitz subcamp]." Here Rudi remained for ten months. Then, in January 1945, in 20-degree weather and with the Soviets advancing quickly toward Auschwitz, the SS packed Rudi and his fellow workers into a score of unheated cattle cars bound for Buchenwald. "This journey continued twelve days . . . without food. By the time we arrived at Buchenwald more than half were perished from cold."[3]

From Buchenwald, the Germans sent Rudi to another Siemens camp: Siemenstadt, near Berlin, where he stayed until mid-February 1945. After repeated bombings rendered Siemenstadt useless, the Nazis brought most of the Siemenstadt prisoners to the Sachsenhausen concentration camp. Finally, in April 1945 (just as the Allies began their final push to take Berlin), Rudi's captors ushered him and more than four hundred fellow prisoners, most of them Russian and French, on a forced march toward a concentration camp in the town of Schwerin. This move brought Rudi and his compatriots away from the advancing Russians but nearer to the advancing Americans. Walking for ten days without shoes and with little food or water, Rudi watched as the SS shot any prisoner who broke down along the line of march. The last day of Rudi's bondage, and the last day of that torturous 140-mile hike, was April 21, 1945, which also happened to be Rudi's twenty-first birthday.

As one of the few German-speaking prisoners, Rudi could understand the conversations—and sense the desperation—of the SS guards as the Allies increased their chokehold around German forces. Given all he had experienced in recent years, he was hardly surprised when, early on the morning of the twenty-first, an SS officer in a staff car stopped by the roadside and told those on guard to take their prisoners into the woods and shoot them. Afterward, the SS men would be free to change into civilian clothes and melt into the landscape. Their war would be over.

Rudi realized there was little time to spare. He immediately turned to three Soviet soldiers walking near him and did his best to describe what he had heard using the limited Russian at his disposal. Confronted with almost certain death unless they acted immediately, the four men jumped the nearest guard, overpowered him, and darted into the brush. After running for several miles, Rudi and the Russians stumbled into a small group of German regular army soldiers who, astonishingly, did not raise a hand to them. Perhaps as a show of disdain for the SS, or perhaps in recognition of the war's undeniable loss, the Germany infantrymen gave the escaped prisoners food and then pointed them in the direction of approaching American tanks.

Later that same day, the Americans escorted the former prisoners to a place in the woods where the machine-gunned corpses of their fellow captives lay. Near that same site, Rudi and the Russians helped the Americans identify several SS guards now dressed in civilian clothes. The Russians were disappointed, however, when the Americans did not immediately execute the former SS, instead taking them into custody "pending trial." Infuriated, the Russians soon broke away from the American units, Rudi going with them for lack of anyplace better to be. "They took off," says a longtime Michigan friend of Bob Felder's, "and the next SS guard the Russians found they tortured to death." This, however, proved to be too much for Rudi, who parted with the Russians and eventually found his way back to Gouda.[4] "Even after all the SS had done to him," says Bob's son, Les Felder, "he couldn't kill them. He couldn't take a life. He told me that he just didn't have the hatred."[5]

At Gouda, Rudi found shelter with a Dutch Christian family who had been friendly with his parents, and soon he got a job at the same machine shop where he had been employed before his 1942 arrest.[6] He returned to work in late May. Shortly thereafter, he met and began courting Gerri. He seemed intent on picking up the pieces of his life, moving on and embracing the future.

Rudi's brother Martin, meanwhile, had been active in the U.S. armed forces. By war's end he was on assignment as a translator in Frankfurt, and it was while in Frankfurt that he received word—via their uncle back in Cleveland, who had received a letter from Rudi—that his young brother had emerged from the war alive. Thus Martin surprised Rudi, whom he had not seen in eight years, at the machine shop one day that July. "They were not in private," says Gerri. "There were lots of workers all around. So they were very unemotional when they first met. They just looked at each other. Later on they hugged and talked about their parents, and the younger brother relayed all the horrors of his experiences."[7] In the ensuing weeks, Martin made several visits—at one point arriving in a jeep loaded down with delicacies of the type that were in short supply outside military circles. It was also at about this time that Martin took Rudi to the American consulate in Amsterdam where they filed the necessary papers for Rudi's immigration to the United States.

Rudi's visa came through two years later. He would never again return to Europe. When he parted with Gerri, he did so with the understanding that he would send for her soon. Rudi traveled by plane to New York where his brother met him and told him straight off he must change his name. Martin had long since shortened and Americanized the family name to Felder; Rudi should do the same. Also, just like Dingfelder, the first name Rudi sounded far too ethnic. From now on he should be Robert (Bob) Felder. That, as the Americans said, was the ticket.[8]

Martin lived in Michigan, where Bob also moved. Gerri joined him in 1948. In a simple ceremony with just Martin and his wife as witnesses, Bob and Gerri married within weeks of her arrival in the United States, and Gerri soon became pregnant. There would eventually be two children, Les and Joanne, to whom Bob proved a loving and devoted father. Bob persevered in his career. Starting at his old profession as a toolmaker, he worked his way up at various Detroit-area firms, eventually becoming a draftsman, a design engineer, and an engineering estimator. "He did not go as far as some of the others with whom he worked," Gerri recalls, "because he did not have a degree. That luxury had been taken away from him by the circumstances of the Holocaust. If it had not been for all of that, he would most certainly have gone to a university for engineering. But he knew his job better than most, better than some with the degrees even. He was a very intelligent man, my Bob."[9]

Five years after his arrival in the United States—as soon as he was allowed by statute—Bob Felder became a citizen of the United States. "That was a very proud day for him," Gerri remembers. "He said the United States was the first place where he ever felt truly free. It annoyed him when people took the United States for granted, when they bad-mouthed the country or made petty complaints. He would say: 'You are spoiled. You do not realize how good you have it here, how wonderful this freedom is.'"

"My father was a total American," says Bob's son, Les. "There was never a prouder American." Only once does Les remember his father mentioning how the United States turned its back on the Dingfelder family in 1939. And this he did mildly, in an almost offhand manner, marrying his criticism with a compliment. He told his son that the United States may not have done right by Rudi Dingfelder, but that it had done more than right by Bob Felder. And this, in the end, seems to have made all the difference.

7

It Depends What You Mean by "Survived"

About the same time that publicity through the NPR report yielded critical leads regarding Rudi Dingfelder, an article about Sarah and Scott's research that appeared in the *Cleveland Plain Dealer* led the team to vital information on yet another *St. Louis* veteran: Recha Weiler, the widow of Moritz Weiler, the passenger who died at sea as the *St. Louis* sailed to Havana.

One day after the list of unaccounted-for passengers appeared in the *Plain Dealer* article, Scott's phone rang. The caller was a doctor in Ohio who told Scott that her grandmother had been a *St. Louis* passenger. "Recha Weiler. Do you know who she was?" Scott replied that he certainly did. In fact, documentation in the National Archives suggested that Mrs. Weiler came to the United States in 1946. "We know that your grandmother survived the war, but we would like to know more of her story." "Survived?" said the caller. "Well, it depends what you mean by 'survived.'" Then she told her grandmother's tale.

Sent to Belgium after the *St. Louis*'s return to Europe, Mrs. Weiler spent most of the war hiding in the home of a Jewish couple who somehow—either by masquerading as non-Jews or through some other device—managed to evade detection by the Nazis. In 1942, when the Nazis started deporting Jews from Belgium, Recha stopped going out of doors. Her "protectors" requested money from Fred Weiler, Recha's son in the United States, claiming the requested funds were needed to obtain medications for his mother's glaucoma and other ailments. Whether

Recha and Moritz Weiler in Germany before the voyage of the *St. Louis*.
(USHMM, courtesy of Ellen L. Payner)

or not the drugs were ever purchased, eventually Mrs. Weiler went blind. She did, however, manage to live through to the war's end. Finally, in 1946, her son sent money to the couple sheltering her, requesting that they book Mrs. Weiler's travel to the United States. A little later on he sent even more money after receiving word that she was too ill to travel alone and that the couple would have to accompany her.

Mrs. Weiler made the journey by plane. Waiting to meet her at the airport in New York, her son and grandchildren became anxious when she did not deplane with the other passengers. Then, finally, they saw her being carried out of the back of the plane on a stretcher. The family was shocked. Mrs. Weiler—dressed very elegantly in a hat, holding her beaded opera bag— appeared to be unconscious. She died a few weeks later, without regaining consciousness. And those accompanying Mrs. Weiler soon departed for parts unknown.

"So, Mr. Miller," concluded the granddaughter, "do you consider Recha Weiler a survivor of the Holocaust? I certainly don't."[1]

Although Mrs. Weiler made it to the United States, in reality she never saw American shores. Technically she was a survivor, but in name only.

8

Reluctant Witness

Not every *St. Louis* passenger wanted to be found. Such was the case with one of the few refugees not from Germany or Austria, a man we shall call Bela in order to guard his privacy. Beyond the fact that Bela was born in Szolnok (Azolnok), Hungary, on November 8, 1913, and lived in Budapest immediately before the voyage, Sarah and Scott knew very little about him. The affidavit accompanying his U.S. visa application bore the signature of a Mrs. Henrik Mayer, who in 1939 lived at 860 East Sixteenth Street in the Bronx but proved untraceable in the 1990s. Following the ship's return to Europe, Bela was sent to France, at which point his paper trail ended.

Sarah and Scott considered Bela unaccounted for until Scott received a terse, anonymous voicemail message on the Wednesday before Thanksgiving in 1998. "The Bela you are looking for," said a calm, slightly accented male voice, "is alive and lives in Connecticut." But the voice offered no elaboration and no means of contact. One sentence only, then a click and a dial tone.

Scott wondered if this could be true. The Museum's search of immigration records at the National Archives had turned up no Bela. But the immigration records are often cryptic and incomplete, so the absence of Bela from those files was by no means proof-positive that he had not entered the United States at some point.

When a check of the phonebook revealed no Bela, Scott used the Museum's voicemail identification system to obtain the telephone number associated with his tipster—a number in New

York City's 212 area code. "My mysterious caller seemed a bit surprised that I was able to reach him," Scott remembers. "I was clearly the last person he was expecting to hear from. He responded guardedly and curtly and explained that he could not talk to me for long because he was at his office." When Scott asked the gentlemen if he was sure his Bela was the one from the *St. Louis,* he answered emphatically: "Of course. Yes. I'm absolutely positive. I talk to Bela all the time. I see him five days a week at work." *At work?* The Bela of the *St. Louis* would have been eighty-five years old in 1998. How many eighty-five-year-olds held full-time jobs, commuting daily between Connecticut and Manhattan? "It is true," the man insisted, as if he had read Scott's mind and heard his unspoken doubts. "Bela still works; and he is eighty-five!" The informant went on to say that he himself was a Holocaust survivor, a German Jew, and a reader of New York's German-language Jewish newspaper *Aufbau,* where a recent article had detailed the Museum's project and listed the unaccounted-for passengers.

Bela—who, the gentleman reminded Scott, was not a *Yekke* (a name used by eastern European Jews for describing German Jews)—had already left the office for the weekend. He would have to be reached at his home. When Scott mentioned that he had been unable to find Bela listed in the phonebook, the informant expressed surprise and said perhaps Bela's number was unlisted. Then, pausing a moment to flip through his Rolodex, the informant rattled off the necessary digits.[1]

Within an hour, Scott found himself on the line with Bela. The old man's voice was congenial, weary, and draped in a thick Hungarian accent. "When I asked if he was the man who had sailed on the *St. Louis,* a good fifteen seconds elapsed before he finally answered quite tentatively and hesitatingly: 'Yes, that was me.'" Bela went on to explain that over the years he had steadfastly avoided contact with anyone who was on the *St. Louis.* Indeed, he had also shunned the wider Holocaust survivor community generally. "This," he said, "was on purpose. I have my reasons."[2] Bela did not seek publicity; he was not interested in reunions. Outside of his friend at work, he had never spoken to anyone about "these terrible things." If he told Scott his story, it would have to be on condition that his anonymity be protected.

Jews had been residents of Hungary for many generations. By the late nineteenth century, many Jews had become well-to-do intellectuals, professionals, and merchants, proud patriots who regarded Hungary as their homeland. Bankers, industrialists, economists, scholars, engineers, and inventors swelled the ranks of Hungary's Jewish community, as did writers, poets, artists, and actors. Such was the world into which young Bela was born, a world that would begin to disintegrate in short order.

During 1919, some three thousand Jews died in the "White Terror," a series of pogroms that followed the overthrow of the briefly installed Communist regime headed by Bela Kun, a Hungarian Jew. Six-year-old Bela's father was among the victims. In March 1938, as part of an effort to head off the growing influence of Hungary's Nazi-inspired Arrow Cross Party, Prime Minister Kálmán Darányi proposed a series of legislative restrictions against the Jews as a means of "solving the Jewish problem" through a "better balance" in Hungary's social and economic life. Thus the First Jewish Law, adopted that year, set strict limits on Jewish participation in Hungary's economy.

Next, a government order dated January 9, 1939, forced all of Hungary's main Jewish newspapers to close down, and by May 1939 the Hungarian legislature had passed the Second Jewish Law, which openly targeted the Jewish community with a number of restrictive measures. Ultimately, the Third Jewish Law, passed in 1941, would define Jewish identity according to the Nuremberg Laws and prohibit any form of intermarriage. Later, yet another statute, implemented in July 1942, annulled the official status of the Jewish community, thereby depriving Jewish institutions of government support while also prohibiting conversion to Judaism.

Despite all this and the fact that Hungary was an ally of Nazi Germany, Jewish life there remained relatively intact in comparison with other countries under the direct authority of the Nazis. For this reason, shortly before the German invasion of western Europe in May 1940, Bela's two brothers were able to convince him to leave France, where he had been sent after the *St. Louis*'s return to Europe, and come home. "After all," Bela told Scott, "people knew the Nazis could invade France at any time, but Hungary? Hungary seemed out of all danger."

Upon returning to his native land, Bela soon found himself conscripted, along with more than 130,000 other Jewish men, into the Jewish labor battalions of the Hungarian army. These sparsely supplied units spent days repairing roads, clearing forests, digging trenches, and building tank traps. The work was often treacherous, and the food was usually scarce. Somewhere between 30,000 and 40,000 battalion personnel died in the course of their service. Bela was among the fortunate. He survived two terms of conscription (in 1940 and 1942, respectively) and never regretted his decision to leave France. During the same periods when Bela worked in the labor battalions, the Jews of France were being systematically deported to Auschwitz by the tens of thousands. (When speaking to Scott, Bela refused to detail the specific tasks he had been assigned and the places he had visited with the battalions as being "too emotional for me.")

After his second tour of duty, Bela returned to his home in Budapest, where he remained on March 19, 1944, the date the German Army occupied Hungary. The situation of the country's Jews deteriorated rapidly. The Germans and the Arrow Cross ordered the nearly 200,000 Jews of Budapest into more than two thousand buildings marked with the Star of David. And from the provinces, the Germans deported more than 440,000 Jews within the first three months of Nazi occupation. By the end of the war nearly 565,000 Jews from Hungarian territory (out of a population of roughly 825,000, which includes converts and Christians of Jewish origin) would be dead.

Bela's brothers, who had believed Hungary to be a safe haven, together with his mother and sixteen other relatives all perished. As for Bela, he survived by going underground. Protected by a forged baptismal certificate, he posed as a Christian and hid his Jewish identity until the day in February 1945 when the Soviets liberated Budapest. Thereafter, Bela rejoined the city's greatly diminished Jewish community and watched to see what would happen next.

The postwar Hungarian regime abolished the anti-Jewish legislation enacted by its predecessor government. A number of the men who had ruled during the war—many of them directly responsible for the deportation and destruction of entire Jewish communities—were brought to trial and sentenced to death. Thousands of other Hungarian war criminals were sent to prison. However, no comprehensive law was passed for the restitution of Jewish property. Likewise, though anti-Semitism was officially banned, a strong strain of anti-Jewish sentiment remained in the general population. There were several pogroms immediately after the war. Even after these ceased, popular anti-Semitism continued, finding expression in acts such as the desecration of cemeteries.

The transformation of Hungary into a Communist state in 1945 represented a fateful turning point. The effects of this move were felt in the economic situation of the Jews, in their public life, and in their educational activities. The nationalization of key industries, agencies, and services deprived large sections of the Jewish population of their means of livelihood. As well, the new regime curtailed and eventually banned all Zionist activities.

Bela foresaw Hungary's Communist future a year before it was fully realized and chose to leave while he could. Departing Budapest in 1948, he made his way to France, where he at first registered for a visa into Paraguay. Then, changing his plans, he immigrated to the United States and settled in Connecticut.

Here Bela ended his story. Despite Scott's gentle prodding, the man refused to divulge any more information. "I tried pressing him and even offered to have a Hungarian-speaking colleague contact him, but he politely refused." Bela said he did not feel the details of his postwar life would be of use or interest to other people. Also, he did not want to spend any more time than was necessary dwelling on the Holocaust. "It's just easier," he concluded, "for me not to talk about it."

9

Shadows

Radio and television news stories along with newspaper accounts of the Museum's research into the fates of *St. Louis* passengers continued to bear fruit throughout 1998, most often in the form of contacts from descendants and other relatives. One such news story led to an e-mail Scott received within weeks of his and Sarah's first contacts with the families of Rudi Dingfelder and Recha Weiler. The message came from Martin Goldsmith, the well-known host of National Public Radio's popular music program *Performance Today.*

"My grandfather, Alex Goldschmidt, and my uncle, Helmut Goldschmidt, were both passengers on the *St. Louis,*" the message read. "You've probably come across at least the name Alex, since the Holocaust Museum has a record of his transport from a camp in France to Drancy and then to Auschwitz. His son Helmut, on the other hand, has an incomplete record. The International Red Cross traced him to France but there is no evidence of his whereabouts after that. Perhaps he died there; there is no evidence of his having been transported to Auschwitz."[1]

Martin Goldsmith's parents, Gunther Goldschmidt, a flutist, and Rosemarie Gumpert, a violist, met and fell in love during the mid-1930s while performing in the Berlin orchestra of the Jewish Kulturbund (Jewish Cultural Association), an organization sponsored by Joseph Goebbels's Ministry of Public Enlightenment and Propaganda.[2] Martin's mother was a second-generation musician whose father, Julian Gumpert, ran a conservatory of his own founding in Düsseldorf. It was there at the conservatory, on the morning after Kristallnacht, that old Mr. Gumpert, joined by

Helmut and Alex Goldschmidt before the voyage of the *St. Louis.* (USHMM, courtesy of Martin Goldsmith)

his daughter and future son-in-law, insisted on playing Beethoven's "Trio for Flute, Violin and Viola." According to Gunther's recollection many years later, Rosemarie's father seemed to be in denial about the atrocities of the previous twelve hours. Mr. Gumpert, Gunther remembered, had insisted that Kristallnacht was just an aberration concocted by "a few drunken idiots" and that the violence would "blow over very soon." Thus his insistence on something profound and eternal: music. "In my house, music comes first," he asserted. "Beethoven will endure when all these fools are forgotten."[3]

As Gunther Goldschmidt played with his fiancée and her father in Düsseldorf, his own father was being rounded up along with other Jewish men in the Goldschmidts' hometown of Oldenburg. Martin remembered:

> Fifty-four years later, in 1992, the year I turned forty, I was visiting Europe. My mother was dead by that time, and my father was living on the Continent. We arranged to meet in the town of his childhood, sort of a middle-sized town in northwest Germany, and he showed me a few things that he remembered from

his childhood: the house where he grew up, and the place where his father Alex had once operated a very successful women's clothing store before the Nazis drove him out of business with a boycott. My father also showed me the *Pferdemarkt*, the horse market, where his father had been taken following his arrest after Kristallnacht. And slowly these shadows—like my grandfather Alex Goldschmidt and my Uncle Helmut, as well as others whom I'd never known—began to take on a bit more human form, and I began to ask a few more questions.

This was new ground for Martin, and painful ground for his father. "As was the case with many families in our situation, my parents didn't talk about what had happened to them or what had happened to their families in Nazi Germany. It was just too painful. So when my father and I finally had these conversations, it was a real watershed."[4]

Following his arrest after Kristallnacht, Alex Goldshmidt wound up being detained briefly at the Sachsenhausen concentration camp. Then the Nazis released him on receipt of a promise that he would take immediate steps to emigrate from Germany. Following his release, Alex and his younger son, Helmut, purchased tickets for the *St. Louis*. Rosemary's father, Julian, meanwhile, reappraised his initial belief that German persecution of the Jews would soon "blow over." He applied for a visa to enter Ecuador and traveled there by plane, intending to send for his wife shortly; but within days of his arrival he died of a heart attack.

"When Alex and Helmut departed on the *St. Louis* in May of 1939," says Martin Goldsmith, "my parents were there waving them off from the dock at Hamburg. At the time, it seemed like my grandfather and uncle had their safety secured, and that my parents—who were still involved with the orchestra in Berlin— were being left to uncertainty. Likewise, my grandmother, Toni Goldschmidt, and her daughter Eva were left behind in Germany, with the promise that my grandfather would send for them once he'd established himself in Cuba."[5] When the *St. Louis* returned to Europe, Alex and Helmut found themselves among those passengers assigned to France. As for Gunther and Rosemarie, a chance encounter with an American diplomat in Berlin during a Jewish Kulturbund concert eventually enabled them to acquire U.S. visas in the spring of 1941. Shortly thereafter they traveled to New York, where they established themselves as Gunther and Rosemarie Goldsmith.

"I hope that you will have soon completed your journey across the big pond and that it will have been, in spite of everything, relaxing and beautiful for you after all the strenuous see-saw days of your emigration." So wrote Alex Goldschmidt to Gunther and Rosemarie on June 19, 1941. Goldschmidt addressed his letter from the Rivesaltes camp in the Pyrenees, where he and Helmut had been interned since May 1940, and where conditions steadily declined under the collaborationist Vichy government. "I wish you, with all my heart, a full measure of happiness and may all your hopes and plans be fulfilled. I must tell you that we don't have anything to wear with the exception of a casual suit, nor even underwear or shoes. . . . I know it would be a crime, after what we have gone through . . . to await the end of the war here if there is any alternative."[6]

Soon Alex wrote again from Rivesaltes. "I am *sure* that you are doing *everything,* in your power to get affidavits for Mother and Eva *as quickly as possible,* so that I can hope to see you all once more in the not-too-distant future. It is this thought that keeps me going and continues to keep me going. When we sailed off on May 13, 1939, on the *St. Louis* and you waved to us for such a long time from the dock, we could not have had an inkling that our voluntary separation would become such a long and involuntary one."[7] Rations were in short supply. According to Alex's letter, both he and Helmut had now, after close to fourteen months in the Rivesaltes camp, lost a full third of their original body weights. Nevertheless, despite nearly constant hunger, twenty-year-old Helmut worked as a medical orderly in the hospital barracks. In this capacity he routinely removed corpses—sometimes as many as three a day, all victims of prolonged undernourishment—to make way for new patients.

The Vichy French transferred Alex and Helmut to Camp Les Milles, located at the site of an abandoned brick factory twelve miles northwest of Marseilles, in early September 1941. "On this New Year's morning," Alex wrote on Rosh Hashanah, September 22, 1941, "I'm sitting on my bed, using my blanket as a desk." Even though they were now out of the mountains and in a somewhat more temperate zone, he and Helmut faced their third winter in France "with quite a bit of horror. The food here is better than it was in Rivesaltes, but it's very unbalanced and contains little fat. . . . There are about thirteen hundred people here, most of whom want to go to the U.S. There are repeated delaying tactics, and the moment the U.S. enters the war everything will come to a stop. . . . I think the worst of the horror is still to come. . . . One must not think about it, and so work is the best medicine."[8] In fact, though Alex did not realize it, everything with regard to U.S. visas had pretty much already come to a stop.

Between the Jewish New Year and the end of 1941, Alex's pessimism increased. The United States formally entered the war in December 1941. Alex turned sixty-three on January 1, 1942. "Yesterday morning," Alex wrote on January 2, "Helmut, who is still my best friend as he has been from the start, gave me for my birthday half a day's ration, ca. 110 grams of bread, an orange, and a fountain pen bought with the pay he just received for work performed . . . at Rivesaltes. He was very dear and made the day really festive. . . . I will bless the day that brings us freedom again. At my age, every month spent under the current conditions shortens one's life; and it is time that the portals to freedom be opened for us. . . . Therefore, do everything you can to get us out."[9]

Helmut endeavored to make the best of his time. Given the large number of artists, musicians, and academics interned at Les Milles, the camp boasted an active cultural life. Helmut took courses in Spanish, bookbinding, European intellectual history, and U.S. history. He also read the plays of Shakespeare, along with Tolstoy's *War and Peace*.[10] In May 1942 Alex wrote Gunther and Rosemarie that he had recently received word from neighbors in Oldenburg that his wife, Toni, and daughter Else had been dispatched "on a long trip." Unbeknownst to Alex, this "trip" was deportation to the east, to a ghetto in Riga, where they perished.[11]

"Perhaps we shall receive the long awaited visa!" Helmut wrote on June 9. "Father is counting on it. Oh, what stories we could tell you then! I'm sure I don't have to emphasize that Father and I help each other out whenever we can and on the whole we are good friends. That's all for today. Next time I'll write more!"[12]

As both Martin Goldsmith and Museum researchers were aware from available documentation, Alex Goldschmidt was among more than 270 Jews ordered to assemble in the courtyard of the Les Milles internment camp on the morning of August 10, 1942. Once gathered, the Jews boarded freight cars destined for the Drancy transit camp. Three days later, Alex joined 1,013 other Jews on yet another train, this one bound from Drancy to Auschwitz. On arrival at Auschwitz, 875 men, women, and children—Alex likely among them—went immediately to the gas chambers.

But what of Helmut? To learn the fate of this young man, Sarah and Scott turned to the Jewish community, the Gemeinde, of Oldenburg. In late 1998, they contacted the president of the Gemeinde, Werner Vahlenkamp, who replied with a surprising fact: Red Cross records showed Helmut as being with his father, Alex, on the convoys to Drancy and Auschwitz. "This was puzzling," remembers Scott, "because our initial search of Red Cross records did not yield this information. We searched again, this time looking for any Goldschmidts from Oldenburg (which we did not do initially because Goldschmidt is such a common name). Sure enough, we found a Goldschmidt from Oldenburg who, like Helmut, was born on September 14, 1921, and who was deported from Drancy to Auschwitz on August 14, 1942, in the same convoy as Alex." The only difference was that *this* Goldschmidt had been listed by the name Klaus. With this piece of information all began to fall into place, as Scott and Sarah realized, and Martin Goldsmith confirmed, that the full name of the young man they were searching for, Helmut Goldschmidt, was Klaus Helmut Goldschmidt.

Selected for labor, Klaus Helmut Goldschmidt received tattoo number 59305. As recorded in the Auschwitz Death Book (under his full name of Klaus Helmut Goldschmidt), he died of "typhoid fever" two months later on October 9. Ten days after Helmut's death, the Nazis deported his mother, Toni, and sister Eva from the Lublin work camp to the Jewish ghetto in Riga, Latvia, after which they were never heard from again. Rosemarie Goldsmith's mother, the widow of Julian Gumpert, likewise died at the hands of the Nazis.

10

Frankfurt-on-the-Hudson

Through the end of 1998 and into early 1999, Sarah and Scott accounted for dozens more *St. Louis* refugees. Two and a half years after beginning their journey, the researchers had determined the fate of all but thirty-five passengers. With the sixtieth anniversary of the sailing of the ship fast approaching on May 13, 1999, they set themselves a goal of tracing the remaining histories by that symbolic date. In the end, Sarah and Scott would not meet their self-imposed deadline, though they would come close.

In this latter phase of the project, Sarah and Scott continued to operate on the assumption that unaccounted-for passengers were survivors. And despite the fact that the names of the thirty-five missing passengers had not shown up in immigration records at the National Archives, they decided to play a hunch that at least some of the people in question might well have found their way to New York, the American city that hosted the largest concentration of postwar Jewish refugees.

With this thought in mind, Scott made a visit to the New York Public Library on Fifth Avenue during the early spring of 1999. "I hoped to get some leads on the missing thirty-five passengers by combing the pages of vintage Manhattan telephone books," he recalls. "Knowing that some of the passengers were probably able to obtain U.S. visas just months after their forced return to Europe in 1939, I began by comparing our remaining thirty-five passenger names to listings in the phone books for that year and continued into the 1960s."

Scott very quickly got some tentative "hits," though, of course, it was impossible to confirm that the Moses Hammerschlag listed at 728 West 181st Street in 1946 was the Moses Hammerschlag of the *St. Louis*, or whether the Freida Gross who lived at 610 West 150th Street after the war was the same young woman who sailed on the *St. Louis* with her sister Johanna. Nevertheless, the addresses that Scott's search turned up resulted in an epiphany. They were all between 140th and 205th Streets on Manhattan's upper west side, Washington Heights, once known popularly as Frankfurt-on-the-Hudson. Suddenly, what should have been obvious all along to Scott, who grew up close to this German Jewish refugee enclave, became clear. He had never before thought of looking in his own childhood backyard for clues on *St. Louis* passengers, but now his recollections of this neighborhood made him realize it quite likely held at least a few of the remaining answers he and Sarah were looking for.

Nearly thirty thousand German Jews had settled in Washington Heights during and after the Holocaust, creating a unique community wherein they preserved their Jewish identity while at the same time fostering a culture that was highly German in its tastes, sensibilities, and habits. Unlike a number of other German Jews who settled elsewhere in New York, many in Washington Heights tended to be religiously observant. By 1999, the German Jewish generation that had first made its home in the Heights was dying out, many of the sons and daughters of that generation having long before become professionals and moved to the suburbs. Now Washington Heights was a neighborhood in transition and was shared by two cultures: a German Jewish minority and a Hispanic majority.[1]

"Washington Heights was close to where I grew up," says Scott, "and its streets and people were very familiar to me. I took the A train from the New York Public Library to 178th Street. Exiting onto the busy Washington Heights corner of 178th Street and Broadway, I realized that this was physically still the neighborhood as I remembered it from my childhood. However, I couldn't help but notice that most of the passers-by were not German Jews, and I wondered if this was really a good idea." But closer inspection revealed some remnants of the old German Jewish community. On West 181st Street, the neighborhood's main shopping and commercial thoroughfare, Scott noticed Gruenbaum's landmark kosher bakery right next door to a Dominican music center and a Spanish-language bookstore.

Seeking a shortcut, Scott decided that the best way to get a barometer of Jewish life in the neighborhood, both past and present, was to visit a synagogue. "So I chose one I knew how to find—Congregation Sha'are HaTikva on 179th Street between Broadway and Amsterdam Avenue." Flanked on one side by an old Episcopal church and on the other by an apartment building, this synagogue, the first such German Jewish establishment to be founded in the Heights, is plainly visible to eastbound drivers on the George Washington Bridge. As if greeting the cars coming into Manhattan, Sha'are HaTikva means Gates of Hope, a name that reflects the aspirations of its founders, all of them refugees from Nazi oppression. Appropriately, Congregation Sha'are HaTikva would also prove a gateway for Scott and Sarah, connecting them to several unaccounted for *St. Louis* passengers and their families.

"But the door to this synagogue was not open to me at first," Scott remembers. "I rang the bell; no one answered, and for a moment I wondered if this was one of the many Washington Heights synagogues that had closed in recent years." Finally, an elderly man wearing a yarmulke and holding a hammer—perhaps, Scott thought, for protection—appeared at the door and, after repeated explanations, allowed Scott to enter. "The man, whom I believed to be the synagogue *shames* [ritual caretaker], looked somewhat puzzled. He asked me, in a German accent, to follow him."

Scott found himself being escorted through an edifice that, though built in the early 1930s, echoed the architecture and expression of German Jewry's past. The sanctuary was adorned with beautiful stained glass. And on one hall leading to the synagogue office hung portraits of the association's past presidents, each bearing quintessentially German Jewish names. Scott reflected that he might have been in any synagogue typical of prewar Germany, save for the prominently displayed plaque that memorialized the destruction of that community.

The office to which the shames led Scott belonged to the synagogue administrator, Reverend Walter Hes, a dignified, elderly gentleman. Sitting down with Scott, Hes, a native of Oldenburg who immigrated to the United States in 1937, listened attentively as the younger man described the nature of his visit. Hes was quick to tell Scott that "if you are looking for information about German Jews, you have come to the right place."

Scott handed Hes a list showing the names of the thirty-five remaining unaccounted-for passengers, along with their places of origin. Scanning the sheet, Reverend Hes immediately noted that his congregation included many people from Berlin, Frankfurt, Furth, Stettin, and more than a dozen other German towns where *St. Louis* passengers had once lived. Subsequently, the reverend agreed to post Scott's list on the synagogue bulletin board and to print it in the Sha'are HaTikva newsletter. Furthermore, he offered to look through old membership lists and burial records to see what he could find.[2] "It may take a while to find the lists," Reverend Hes added, as the records years ago had been placed in the synagogue's attic. "We never thought we would have to retrieve these records," he continued, "as nobody has ever come here asking to see them before."

Scott heard from Reverend Hes several weeks later. The reverend said he had located some synagogue records he thought might be helpful. Scott should come up and have a look.

One week later, on a Friday morning in February 1999, Hes sat Scott and Sarah down in the synagogue's conference room before several boxes of membership lists as well as a large collection of death and burial certificates. "We went through the material carefully," says Scott, "searching for familiar names. And one thing stuck out as we scanned the papers. Usually Jewish religious records, especially synagogue membership records, include the names of the members' parents, their places and dates of birth, and their places and dates of death. The death date is particularly important so that every congregant will know when to say the Kaddish. What was unusual in the membership records of Sha'are HaTikva was the number of question marks in the spaces allocated for parents' dates of death." The places of death were all too clearly delineated—Auschwitz, Sobibór, Gurs—but dates were uniformly unknown. "It became clear," Scott recalls, "that we were looking at the records of not just any American synagogue but one whose members were completely bound up in the tragedy of the Holocaust. Such is the case with virtually every synagogue in Washington Heights."

Sifting through the membership lists and burial certificates, Sarah and Scott spotted a number of familiar surnames from their list of missing passengers, but most of them were too common to be of particular use. "We were," says Scott, "well aware that, as the survivor community aged, we were competing with time; thus, we could not afford to call and check every Lichtenstein and Goldschmidt. We simply had to hold out for more promising leads."

Finally, amid the litany of common German names, Sarah and Scott found a less common one: Hammerschlag. Indeed, here was a certificate documenting the 1947 burial of a gentleman named Moses Hammerschlag in the Sha'are HaTikva plot at Beth El-Cedar Park, Paramus, New Jersey—an exact name match with the *St. Louis* passenger who had been born in Gensungen, Germany, on October 28, 1883. Scott had already found in an old phone book from 1946 the presence of a Moses Hammerschlag living on 181st Street in Washington Heights. The man buried at Beth El-Cedar Park was almost certainly the same individual. But was this the Moses Hammerschlag who had voyaged on the *St. Louis?* From the data on the burial certificate—devoid of a birth date—Sarah and Scott could not tell.

Overall, they knew very little about the Moses Hammerschlag of the *St. Louis*. During 1939 he applied for a U.S. visa at the American consulate in Stuttgart and received the waiting number 13,923. Following the *St. Louis's* return to Europe, he went to Belgium. And there the information on Hammerschlag dried up. Back in 1939, Hammerschlag's visa sponsor had been a Meinhardt Hammerschlag (presumably a relative) who lived on Thirty-fourth Avenue in Jackson Heights, Queens. But by the 1990s Meinhardt was long gone, along with the rest of the once-large German Jewish community of Jackson Heights, which left in the 1950s to make way for other immigrant groups.

Luckily, Hammerschlag's burial certificate provided at least one possible lead: the name of the person who had paid for the grave's perpetual care. This was a Victoria Rosenberg, who lived in Washington Heights and with whom Reverend Hes was acquainted. Reverend Hes immediately called her and put Scott on the phone. "Mrs. Rosenberg, was your uncle Moses Hammerschlag the same Moses Hammerschlag who sailed on the *St. Louis?*" She replied, "Yes, he was."

He was her father's brother. As a young woman she had lived with him. That was back in 1946, she said, right after nine-year-old Victoria, her parents, and her ten-year-old brother immigrated to the United States from Argentina (where the family had fled from Germany). Settling in Washington Heights, they moved into the two-room apartment shared by her Uncle Moses and his son Meinhardt. (Scott recognized the name from the sponsor forms associated with Moses' visa application). Moses, Mrs. Rosenberg recalled, was at the time in very poor health. She remembered that he walked with a cane and was soon confined to a hospital bed that his son set up in the apartment's combination kitchen–living room. He was sixty-four when he died in February 1947 of what Mrs. Rosenberg described on the phone as "a broken heart."[3]

Sarah and Scott were anxious to speak with Victoria Rosenberg at greater length concerning her Uncle Moses and his experiences after the *St. Louis.* "We asked for permission to visit her," Scott remembers, "and she said she would be pleased to have us come over, though she was busy cooking because it was by now Friday afternoon, the Sabbath eve."

Arriving at the Rosenbergs' building, Sarah and Scott looked at the various family names listed on the intercom. Almost all were German Jewish names—Cahn, Hoffman, Schoenberg, Spiegler, Wolf. Inside the apartment, Henry Rosenberg greeted them wearing a yarmulke. Then Mrs. Rosenberg came out of the kitchen with her head covered by a *sheitel* (a woman's wig meant to serve as a sign of modesty in the stricter circles of orthodoxy). Sarah and Scott subsequently learned that the Rosenbergs were members of an Orthodox community known as Breuers or, more formally, K'hal Adath Yeshurun, the scion synagogue of the German rabbinical family headed by Rabbi Joseph Breuer.

The purpose of the Breuers community is to achieve sanctification of all human endeavors, including the secular. Implicit in this is the notion that Jews can be both strictly orthodox and part of the "real world." However, this involvement with the world does not mean compromise with it. The Breuers reject the many delicate compromises—such as not wearing traditional head covering in public—which characterize the modern orthodoxy practiced by other Washington Heights synagogues. During the last few decades there has been a resurgence of Breuers practice in the neighborhood.

Sitting down in her neat living room, Mrs. Rosenberg showed Sarah and Scott a prewar family photo, one that provided a glimpse into the vanished world once inhabited by her Uncle

Moses Hammerschlag (standing) with his family in Kassel, Germany, before
World War II. Moses was the only one in his family to survive the Holocaust.
(USHMM, courtesy of Victoria Rosenberg)

Moses. The photo showed Moses as a smiling young man surrounded by his parents, siblings, nieces, and nephews. Moses
and all the other family members stood dressed in formal yet
modest garb. In a level voice, Victoria explained that a number of
the people in the picture eventually died at the hands of the
Nazis. Her uncle—one of the lucky ones—entered the United
States on March 21, 1940, aboard the SS *Lancastria* at the port of
New York. His exit from Europe came only six weeks before the
German march into Belgium.

Moses received naturalization as a U.S. citizen on December
10, 1945, in New York City, after having spent some five years living with his son Meinhardt, first in Jackson Heights and later in
Washington Heights. According to Mrs. Rosenberg, the son had
been born in Germany in February 1921 and had immigrated to
the United States in 1938, just a few months before the father's
ill-fated voyage on the *St. Louis*. She added that Meinhardt was
now retired and living in Florida. She jotted down his number

Scott and Sarah with Herbert Harwitt in the library of Mount Sinai Jewish Center in New York, March 1999. *(New York Times)*

and suggested that Sarah and Scott call him if they wanted any more details about Moses.[4]

Subsequent telephone discussions with Meinhardt revealed the rest of the Hammerschlag family story. It was very difficult for him to talk to Scott and Sarah, and when they heard his story, it became obvious why. Moses' wife, Miriam, had chosen not to join Moses on the voyage of the *St. Louis;* she instead remained behind in Germany to care for her elderly father. Moses never heard from Miriam after 1942. Only when Meinhardt made a postwar trip to Germany did father and son learn that Miriam had been deported from Germany to Lublin, Poland, on May 12, 1942.[5]

On the same day they visited Reverend Hes and Victoria Rosenberg, Sarah and Scott also paid a call at the Mount Sinai Jewish Center, located just a few doors up from the Rosenberg apartment on Bennett Avenue. There they were greeted by Herbert Harwitt, synagogue administrator and himself a prewar refugee from Germany.

Harwitt's synagogue had as many German Jewish refugees as any other in Washington Heights; thus he guessed that some of his members might recognize names on Sarah and Scott's unaccounted-for list. He himself took a particular interest in Wilhelm Buchholz from Schildberg, Germany, as he was from that town. Standing in his office, Harwitt took out a book describing the history and fate of the Schildberg Jewish community. He showed Sarah and Scott his family's picture, with himself as a child. Then he commented that many in that family photo died at Auschwitz, while the fortunate remainder came to Washington Heights. But the book contained no mention of Buchholz.[6]

Harwitt gave Sarah and Scott access to synagogue membership lists going back twenty years. When the researchers got to the letter M, they found the name Minna Muenz, which resembled the name of unaccounted-for passenger Meta Muenz. Meta, a German name, could very well be Minna in its Jewish form. Harwitt's records indicated that Minna had recently moved uptown, both literally and figuratively, out of Washington Heights to the more upscale Riverdale. Nevertheless, she maintained her synagogue affiliation with the Mount Sinai Jewish Center.

The paper trail on *St. Louis* passenger Meta Muenz was brief. Born in 1912 in the German village of Altengronau, she sailed on the *St. Louis* with her parents and sister. The family wound up in Brussels—specifically, the Jewish refugee neighborhood of Anderlicht—following the *St. Louis*'s return to Europe. When the Germans began their attack on Belgium in May 1940, local police arrested Meta's father, Karl, as an "enemy alien" and transported him to France, where he remained as a prisoner at the St. Cyprien internment camp. Later in the year the French transferred him to Gurs. Conditions in this internment camp were dismal. Many prisoners suffered from malnutrition and typhus. With the help of the JDC, Karl applied for a visa to enter the United States, but he died at Gurs on February 26, 1941, within months of qualifying.

A year and a half after Karl's death, in September 1942, the Gestapo in Brussels rounded up Meta's mother, Sophie, and sister, Paula, and dispatched them to the Mechelen transit camp. One week later, Sophie and Paula were forced to board a convoy bound for Auschwitz. Neither survived the war. Meta, however, remained a mystery. Her name did not show up on the list of Jews taken to Mechelen and then Auschwitz with Sophie and Paula, nor on any other convoy lists. Adding to the mystery, Sarah and Scott had in their possession a mysterious postwar

Sarah, Gay Bamberger, Eva Knoller, and Scott at the Washington Heights office of Selfhelp, February 1999. (USHMM)

Red Cross sheet listing the name Meta Muenz. Stamped "Belgium—Closed," the document revealed nothing of her fate.

"We were anxious to call Minna Muenz right away," says Scott, "but Harwitt seemed hesitant and protective of his congregant." Even if Minna Muenz was not *St. Louis* passenger Meta Muenz, Harwitt knew she was a Holocaust survivor who had lost family in Europe. So, this call in any case would not be simple. Accordingly, he suggested that Sarah and Scott talk to Eva Knoller, a child refugee in the 1930s from Berlin and currently a social worker active in aiding elderly former victims of Nazi oppression. She, he suggested, should be the one to call Minna Muenz.

Eva Knoller served as the director of the Washington Heights Branch of Selfhelp, a social services agency for Holocaust survivors. The clientele of the Washington Heights Selfhelp office was made up almost exclusively of survivors from Germany and German-speaking countries. Knoller understood the German Jewish experience well. Not only was she born in Berlin, but a number of her family members, and those of her husband, were murdered by the Nazis.

At the time of Sarah and Scott's visit, the Washington Heights Selfhelp offices were located at 717 West 177th Street, between Broadway and Fort Washington Avenue. The building, once solidly German Jewish, was now nearly all made up of Dominican residents. Children played in the hallway while their mothers conversed in Spanish and music blared from radios in the background. Inside the offices, Mrs. Knoller showed Sarah and Scott her cabinets crammed with files on hundreds of clients, all Holocaust survivors. Because of their confidential nature, Mrs. Knoller could not open her files to the researchers, but she agreed to go through the papers and look for names from Sarah and Scott's list.

Spending time with Mrs. Knoller, Sarah and Scott were reminded that, sixty years after the Holocaust, all was not well in Washington Heights. The Washington Heights with which Mrs. Knoller dealt was a neighborhood inheriting not only the culture, faith, and religious practices of the prewar Jewish community in Germany but also a range of unresolved issues. Mrs. Knoller explained that the aging Jews of Washington Heights struggled with emotional insecurities and uncertainties arising from the traumas of the past. Composed to a large degree of devout worshipers, the Jewish community of Washington Heights is also one of scarred souls who, though they seek solace through faith in God, nevertheless remain cynical when it comes to mankind. For many, the comfort of America and the relative safety of Washington Heights are not enough to lift the burden of the Holocaust.

Mrs. Knoller's many years of dealing with Holocaust survivors were evident when she picked up the phone to speak with Minna Muenz. Rather than broach her primary subject directly, she chatted with Muenz about her family and Passover plans. Only after these preliminaries did she finally ask if Minna was Meta Muenz from Altengronau and if she had been on the *St. Louis.*[7]

Minna's answer was an emphatic "no." She had not been on the *St. Louis* nor had she ever been called Meta. Anyway, Muenz was her married name. Her late husband, however, did have relatives from Altengronau, a German town that had only the tiniest of Jewish populations (just forty-six individuals) even before the Holocaust. That being the case, Minna suggested that Mrs. Knoller call one of her husband's relatives, Walter Muenz, who also lived in Riverdale.

A subsequent call to Walter Muenz yielded more information. He had been a child in Altengronau and had known Meta, who was not just a relative but also a neighbor. Unfortunately, he had no precise knowledge of what happened to her during the war. He did, however, tell Knoller that Meta had an older brother, Morris (born Moritz), who was not on the *St. Louis* because he had come to the United States by himself a year earlier, in 1938. Morris, Walter believed, was still alive, although he had moved years before from Washington Heights to the more prosperous neighborhood of Forest Hills, Queens.

Knoller quickly found Morris Muenz in the Queens telephone book and called him. When an answering machine picked up, she left a message. The next day she received a telephone call from a Cynthia Muenz of New Paltz, New York. She had retrieved the message from her father Morris's answering machine. Unfortunately, he had died a year earlier at the age of eighty-seven. But Cynthia possessed the information Sarah and Scott required: *St. Louis* passenger Meta Muenz was indeed her father's sister. As to her aunt's fate, Cynthia assumed Meta perished in the Holocaust but did not have any details. She said her father was the only person who claimed to know the complete story of what happened to Meta, but he would never tell anyone. A psychotherapist by training, Cynthia Muenz understood her father's reluctance to speak. "It's somewhat typical," she said. Her father "kept locked inside him whatever he remembered of his slain family," telling her only that they had died "in the camps."[8]

Died in the camps? Sarah and Scott's research through archival sources had found Meta's father, mother, and sister and documented their fates. However, the very fact that their search for Meta continued indicated that they had been unable to find similar documentation for her. Still, death in the Holocaust seemed the most likely truth to be had, since even her own brother had never heard from her again.

Reexamination of the appropriate archives seemed in order. Sarah and Scott turned their focus back to Europe, beginning to weigh the possibility that Meta may have been deported after all, perhaps under a different name. The researchers contacted the archives of the Joods Museum von Deportatie (Jewish Deportation Museum) at Mechelen, located on the site of the infamous transit camp. The Mechelen archives contain the 1942 German registration of Jews in Belgium. Librarians there found no registration form for a Meta Muenz but did discover one filled out under the name of Martha Muenz. The date and place of Martha's birth were recorded as January 28, 1912, in Altengronau, the same as Meta's. Also, Martha's last address in Belgium was exactly the same as that on the registration forms of Sophie and Paula, Meta's mother and sister. Additional documents from the census taken in 1942 showed Martha's parents as Karl and Sophie, with a sister Paula, and confirmed her presence on the same convoy that carried Sophie and Paula to their deaths.

Hammerschlag and Muenz—one who died a broken old man in Manhattan, another who died a young woman at the hands of the Nazis in Europe—represented just the first layer of *St. Louis* information to be found via contacts and connections in Washington Heights. Sarah and Scott's list of unaccounted-for passengers had now been whittled down to thirty-three. In the coming weeks and months, the researchers would make several more key discoveries on the avenues and side streets of Frankfurt-on-the-Hudson, a neighborhood that, as the researchers would find out, to this day plays host to a significant number of *St. Louis* survivors. Indeed, Scott and Sarah would carefully heed Eva Knoller's words uttered near the end of their first meeting with her: "Don't write off this neighborhood."

11

Graveyards

Paramus, New Jersey's Beth El-Cedar Park is a large cemetery with row upon row of graves clustered in groups associated with Jewish societies, most of them based in New York City. A number of older graves, spaced with ample room between them, are covered with green grass. But newer graves added in the last twenty years or so sit in more tightly compressed sections. These graves are most often topped with gravel because the crowded proximity of the gravestones prohibits the growth of grass. The stones throw too many shadows; they also make it impossible to water.

A large, modern building at the center of the cemetery serves multiple purposes. Here visitors find an administrative office, a columbarium (to serve those Reform Jews who choose cremation), and a chapel for committal services. People entering the main foyer of the building turn left to enter the columbarium, go forward to visit the chapel, or turn right to enter the efficient cemetery office.

It was to this office that Scott came the morning of May 13, 1999—coincidentally, the sixtieth anniversary of the *St. Louis's* departure from Hamburg for Havana. Scott had been wrapping up the last leg of a drive from Washington, D.C., to Manhattan when, on impulse, he thought of stopping at Beth El-Cedar Park. "I was still a few miles out from New York," he recalls, "on Route 95 heading in the direction of the George Washington Bridge, when I started seeing signs for Paramus and I remembered Reverend Hes mentioning that Moses Hammerschlag was buried in

Benno Joseph's tombstone in Beth El-Cedar Park Cemetery, Paramus, New Jersey. (USHMM)

Beth El-Cedar Park. I had a little time to spare, so I got off the turnpike and went to the cemetery."

Using her computer, an office attendant looked up "Hammerschlag, Moses." Then she placed an X on a small cemetery map. "But I am terrible with directions," Scott admits. "I wound up stumbling around an area of the cemetery several hundred yards from where I was supposed to be; and while I was looking for Moses Hammerschlag, I came upon the marker for someone else entirely, someone I'd never expected to encounter in Paramus, New Jersey." Benno Joseph was a *St. Louis* passenger Sarah and Scott had previously traced to an Auschwitz subcamp where he worked as a slave laborer and where his paper trail went cold. The likelihood that Joseph, who was forty-eight years old when he was deported, survived the war was slim. "You can imagine how amazed I was when I came across a headstone inscribed Benno Joseph, born January 16, 1894, and died March 27, 1969."

Scott noted down the information and then, still not quite believing what he had seen, moved onward through the many long rows of graves to pay his respects to Moses Hammerschlag.

Later, before departing Beth El-Cedar Park, Scott attempted to get contact information for the family associated with Benno Joseph but found his request denied by Beth El-Cedar Park staffers, who cited cemetery rules governing client confidentiality. "Also," Scott remembers, "the synagogue associated with the group of graves where I'd found Benno Joseph's headstone—Ohav Shalom in Washington Heights—had closed its doors many years before. So I could look for no help there either. The mystery was quite a puzzling one all around, since all the paperwork Sarah and I had previously uncovered left Benno Joseph at the edge of death in 1944. As relieved as I was that Joseph had endured and gone on to settle in New York, I was also desperate to get the rest of his story."

Benno Joseph, his wife Hertha, and their daughter Brigitte were among the *St. Louis* passengers sent to France. French records place them at Camp de Casseneuil in August 1942. From there, on the twenty-sixth, they were dispatched to the Drancy transit camp and then, two weeks later, to Auschwitz.

The Auschwitz convoy on which the Josephs traveled consisted of 1,017 people. When the convoy stopped briefly at Kosel, Germany, the SS removed approximately two hundred men (Benno Joseph among them) for enlistment as forced laborers at the nearby Blechhammer work camp, an industrial complex founded in April 1940 and centered around a large chemical plant. Forty-three-year-old Hertha and eleven-year-old Brigitte remained on the train, however, and were likely among those 707 deportees gassed immediately upon their arrival at Auschwitz.

Joseph was still at the Blechhammer work camp on April 1, 1944, when the camp was placed under the control of the SS and became Arbeitslager Blechhammer. The camp's new commandant, SS Hauptsturmführer Heinrich Schwarz, was also in charge of the Auschwitz III work camp in Monowitz, Poland, of which Blechhammer now became a subcamp. SS records dated April 1 note the assignment of Benno Joseph's prisoner number 177587. Joseph was one of more than three thousand male prisoners enrolled in the new Arbeitslager Blechhammer that day. Those inmates who did not make it past selection to receive a prisoner number were immediately sent to the main Auschwitz killing center.

Benno Joseph's Auschwitz prisoner registration card. (Państwowe Muzeum, Auschwitz-Birkenau)

The number of prisoners at Arbeitslager Blechhammer eventually reached about 5,500, of whom approximately 1,500 died at the camp. (Some prisoners perished in the midst of Allied bombings meant to cripple Blechhammer's industrial capacity. Others succumbed to disease and starvation, while still others were eventually sent to the Auschwitz gas chambers.) On January 25, 1945, as the Allies approached on the ground, the Nazis forced some four thousand prisoners on a long march to the Gross-Rosen concentration camp near Strzegom, in lower Silesia. The death march, conducted on sparse rations through freezing winter weather, took thirteen days. About eight hundred prisoners died en route. Scott and Sarah could hardly imagine Benno Joseph surviving such an ordeal.

Almost one year to the day after Scott happened onto Benno Joseph's New Jersey resting place, he received a letter from the Red Cross International Tracing Service in Bad Arolsen, Germany, carrying unexpected news. It appeared that Benno Joseph had a daughter, Hanna. She lived in Washington Heights and had agreed to be put in touch with the United States Holocaust Memorial Museum.

Scott and Sarah had not previously been aware of a Joseph family daughter named Hanna, but a phone call soon explained things. Hanna turned out to be Benno Joseph's stepdaughter. Now a woman in her sixties with a slight German accent, Hanna fielded Scott's questions warily. She had been seven in 1940 when her biological father, her mother, and she boarded one of the last boats to leave Hamburg. The family settled in Washington Heights, but Hanna's father died soon after their arrival. Hanna's mother, Frieda, subsequently married Benno—then a deliveryman for an egg company—in 1950, when Hanna was seventeen.

Through the years, Hanna continually tried to get Benno to reveal his experiences during the Holocaust, but these he spoke grudgingly. "It was so terrible," he told her. "You should never hear about such things." Benno almost never mentioned his first wife and daughter. After repeated questions from Hanna, he revealed only that he had escaped from Arbeitslager Blechhammer sometime in 1944 and fled eastward into Soviet territory, where he remained until the war ended. Later, once the Nazis were defeated, he traveled to Paris where he, Hertha, and Brigitte had agreed to meet should they become separated. And it was there, in Paris, that Joseph received formal Red Cross notification that his wife and daughter had perished. Shortly thereafter he journeyed to New York, his visa finally approved.

Now knowing that Joseph's story was that of a survivor, Scott wanted to know more about his experiences. He asked Hanna if there was anyone else still alive in whom her stepfather would have confided. "Of course," she exclaimed. And then she revealed that her mother, the second Mrs. Joseph, was still alive. She was one hundred years old and lived in a nursing home in Washington Heights. Frieda Joseph certainly knew more of the details of Benno's story. Speculating, Scott wondered if Frieda might not have heard a more graphic account of life in Arbeitslager Blechhammer from her husband, as well as additional information on his first wife and daughter who perished. Understandably though, Hanna did not want to upset her mother after all these years by probing about her late husband's Holocaust experiences.

We may never know exactly what happened to Benno Joseph during the war. "With his stepdaughter," Scott comments, "we encountered a remnant of memory—close, but not close enough."

Over three thousand miles from Beth El-Cedar Park, an ancient Jewish cemetery lies adjacent to an ornate *taharah* (purification) house decorated with beautiful stained-glass windows. This proud establishment—the remnant of another day, before European Jewry suffered under Hitler's regime—stands near the center of Magdeburg, Germany. As a life-affirming act, and in accordance with Jewish tradition, people wash their hands in this house after leaving the cemetery in order to reenter the community of the living.

A room off to one side houses a large collection of funeral urns. The presence of these urns has been a mystery for several generations of Magdeburg Jews, since Orthodox Judaism does not allow the cremating of the dead. Some speculate that the presence of the urns was, before the rise of the Nazis, a sign of what was to befall the Jews of Magdeburg. More than 1,500 Magdeburg residents wound up in death camps where they were gassed and their bodies incinerated. These victims of the Nazis are memorialized by a monument in front of the *taharah* house. As well, behind the building, there stands a memorial to the more than one million Jewish children killed in Nazi camps.

Like much of Europe, Magdeburg boasts an auspicious Jewish past and only the tiniest sliver of a Jewish present. The first Jews settled here as early as 965, and the town had a Jewish population of 3,200 in 1933. On Kristallnacht in 1938 the city's Moorish-style main synagogue, which sat nine hundred people, was burned to the ground. Today, on Bremerstrasse, at a spot close to where this house of worship once stood, a plaque commemorates the synagogue and the entire Magdeburg Jewish community. The only Jewish institutions remaining in the town are the Gemeinde (Jewish community), the Jewish community center, and a prayer room, all housed in a large villa. A mezuzah affixed to the entrance is the only indication that it is a Jewish building. On the gate an inscription reads *Gott beschütze dieses Haus* (God, protect this house).

The inscription is especially poignant in light of the recent history of Magdeburg Jewry. At the end of World War II, only 185 Jews remained in the town—mainly the partners of mixed marriages. Today, only about one hundred Jews reside there. One of them, I. A. Ledermann, serves as president of the Gemeinde. Ledermann is a Holocaust survivor who, after the war, stayed to help rebuild Magdeburg, confounding those who insisted there could never again be Jewish life in Germany. Thus it was to Ledermann that Scott Miller wrote at the height of the search for information about three Magdeburg residents on the passenger manifest of the *St. Louis:* Viktor Waldbaum, his wife, Margarete, and their two-year-old daughter Gerda.

Sarah and Scott knew that Victor, who owned a confectionery store, was interned at Buchenwald after Kristallnacht, along with many other of Magdeburg's Jewish men. Released a few weeks later on condition that he emigrate, Waldbaum subsequently purchased passage on the *St. Louis* for himself and his family, all of whom went to France once the *St. Louis* returned to Europe. In response to Scott's query concerning the Waldbaums, Ledermann forwarded copies of two letters, both addressed to the "Gemeinde zu Magdeburg" and both authored by none other than Viktor Waldbaum himself. Dated July 20, 1947, and February 12, 1963, respectively, the letters made queries as to the fates of friends and neighbors from Magdeburg. Both had return addresses in Basel,

Switzerland. Neither note made reference to Viktor's wife or daughter, but soon an internet search by Scott revealed a Gerda Waldbaum living at the last known address for Viktor.[1]

A subsequent letter of inquiry from Scott received a prompt response. "I am Gerda Waldbaum," she wrote, "born June 1, 1937, in Magdeburg. My father Victor and mother Margarete and I were passengers on the *St. Louis*."[2] The balance of her note narrated the Waldbaums' flight first from Paris, then from Lyon, and finally from Nice during the summer of 1942, just as the Nazi deportation of Jews from France reached full force.

Hearing that some Jews had fled from southeastern France to safety in Switzerland, Viktor took Margarete and five-year-old Gerda and made the sixty-mile trek, mostly by foot, from Nice to the Swiss Alps. It took the family one week to get to the Alps, after which they still had to hike over the mountains and sneak through barbed wire at the Swiss border. (Being discovered by Swiss border guards would have meant arrest and surrender to French gendarmes or the Gestapo on the French side of the border, as the Swiss were by this time denying entry to refugees from France.) Once safely across the border, Viktor and Margarete spent the remainder of the war in refugee camps near Geneva while their daughter lived with various Christian families in the area. Toward the very end of the war, the family was reunited and interned at a camp near Basel, where they eventually settled.

Viktor Waldbaum, while rejoicing in the survival of his family, nevertheless always mourned his friends and relatives from Magdeburg who did not survive the Holocaust and who vanished without a trace. He died in 1972. His wife, Margarete, died twenty-two years later. Today Gerda Waldbaum, retired from a career in business, lives quietly and alone in her parents' old Basel apartment.

In the United States, precise records and such entrenched and stable artifacts as gravestones served as concrete guideposts to the truth. In Europe, however—even though the entire continent, in the wake of the Holocaust, served as a metaphoric graveyard—signposts were much more vague and indiscernible. With whole communities lost, so too have massive amounts of records, as well as an entire social fabric, disappeared. "We don't have graves over there," says Scott. "And we don't have precise files. We are lucky when we have names. And the Waldbaums— who survived as a cohesive family unit and then turned out to be traceable in the end—are not common at all."

Discovery of Benno Joseph and the Waldbaum family brought Sarah and Scott's unaccounted-for list down to a count of just twenty-nine. They were getting close to the end of their quest, but were not there yet.

12

Cruel Calculus

In the spring of 1999 fifty-eight-year-old Marianne Meyerhoff sat with a Los Angeles–based researcher who was preparing her PhD thesis on the first-born children of Holocaust survivors. Marianne told her story as the researcher earnestly took notes for her ongoing quest into the minds—and, by extension, the hearts—of children of survivors.

Born in Florida in 1941 and raised in the Los Angeles neighborhood of Watts, Marianne's life experience had been that of an American though colored by being the daughter of refugees. The catastrophe in Europe—and what was left behind—hovered over Marianne's childhood. In addition to this, Marianne's father enlisted in the U.S. Army as an interpreter and was sent back to Europe, and was among the first American troops into Berlin. He was gone the whole time Marianne was growing up. As far as growing up in America was concerned, German Jews, she recalled, "were not all that well received in the community by Jews and Christians alike. To add a little vignette to this point, I thought all the other children in America were blond and blue eyed and had families like Ozzie and Harriet."

Marianne's parents, Warren and Charlotte, were married in Berlin on December 16, 1938, in a small ceremony at her parents' apartment. And that very evening he left town, bound for Cuba. Charlotte followed soon thereafter in May, departing Hamburg on "a ship" that was turned away at Havana, eventually returning to Europe.

"That must have been the *St. Louis*," said the researcher, a longtime member of the United States Holocaust Memorial

Charlotte Meyerhoff on board the *St. Louis*, May/June 1939. (USHMM, courtesy of Marianne Meyerhoff)

Museum. "I have something that will interest you though I am sure it will upset you." From the top of a pile of papers she retrieved the latest issue of the *Update,* the Museum's newsletter, which featured a piece on Sarah and Scott's project. "In Search of *St. Louis* Passengers," read the headline. Scanning the *Update*'s listing of unaccounted-for refugees, Marianne quickly found her mother's name.

One day later, Marianne spoke on the phone for more than an hour with Scott, telling him the details of her family's story and in the process helping him bring the number of names on the unaccounted-for list down to twenty-eight.[1]

Interned at Westerbork by the Dutch after the *St. Louis* returned to Europe, Charlotte found herself suddenly rescued one night by a "mystery man" who tossed a blanket over her head and then smuggled her out of the camp. Charlotte never knew for certain the identity of her savior, though she thought it might have been a family friend from Amsterdam who wielded some influence. Then, early in 1940, just months before the German invasion of the Netherlands, Charlotte was able to arrange passage to Cuba on a cargo ship.

Warren and Charlotte lived in Havana for several months before migrating to the United States. When Marianne was born in 1941, Charlotte's parents, still in Berlin, sent a letter of congratulations. This would be one of the last times Charlotte would hear from her mother and father, both of whom were deported later that year. Once the United States entered World War II, Warren enlisted in the U.S. Army and fought in Europe. When he returned from the war, he opened a woodworking firm while Charlotte pursued a career as a nurse. The couple divorced in 1947.

Charlotte Meyerhoff's circuitous route to the United States had made tracking her through conventional means nearly impossible. From the perspective of the records Sarah and Scott routinely accessed in their quest for data on *St. Louis* passengers, the last formal documentation of Charlotte was her incarceration by the Dutch at Westerbork. Cash payment travel on a cargo vessel leaves little paper trail. Thus it was only through serendipity—Charlotte's daughter telling her story to the right person at the right time—that a connection was made.

During October 1999, Sarah and Scott visited Marianne at her home in the canyons of Los Angeles. There they sifted through

Charlotte and Warren Meyerhoff reunited at a coffee plantation near Havana, Cuba, 1940. (USHMM, courtesy of Marianne Meyerhoff)

boxes containing a rich collection of prewar belongings and photographs left to Marianne by Charlotte, who had died more than a decade before. Many of the photos showed Charlotte as a child in Berlin with her friends, a large number of whom were not Jewish. As Sarah and Scott studied the images, Marianne mentioned how her mother once said that all the girls in the photos, Jew and Christian alike, felt equally German and at home in Berlin during the 1920s and early 1930s.

Ironically, the very fact that these artifacts rest today in California, and were not themselves lost in the Holocaust, represents a legacy of German Jewish symbiosis that no longer exists. The photos and memorabilia that Marianne now treasures were salvaged from the home of Charlotte's parents by one of Charlotte's childhood friends, a non-Jew. Once a week the girl would visit, using the pockets in the lining of her oversized trench coat to smuggle in fruit and other commodities forbidden to Jews. Then, upon leaving, she would fill the same coat with photo albums and other precious family heirlooms. Preparing for the worst, Charlotte's father had asked the young woman, named Erika, to safeguard these possessions for the daughter he feared he would never see again.

At this point in their project, Sarah and Scott had been giving many public presentations on their research. They did this in part to educate a wider audience about the *St. Louis* and partially because they hoped that people who heard the story of the search might be able to help fill in blanks about missing passengers. Thus, after visiting Marianne Meyerhoff, the two researchers drove to the nearby University of Judaism in Los Angeles to give a talk to a large group.

At the end of their presentation, as Sarah and Scott packed up their slides and notes, a dignified, soft-spoken gentleman in his sixties approached. Identifying himself as Peter Heiman of Malibu, he explained that he and his parents had been friends with a *St. Louis* family, the Dublons, back in Erfurt, Germany. The Dublons—Willi and Erna and their daughters Lore and Eva and Willi's brother Erich—had all been sent to Belgium after the *St. Louis*'s return to Europe and had not survived the war. "Lore was my girlfriend," Heiman said. "We went to kindergarten and we played together frequently. The Dublons owned a shoe store called Salamander Schuhe. We used to go on hikes with them every Sunday and they attended many parties at my parents' house."

Unlike the Dublons, the Heiman family managed to get to the safety of North America. They were living in New York City by April 1940, where they occasionally received correspondence from Willi Dublon in Brussels. In one happy, gossipy note, Willi jokingly described the wonderful presents he had for the Heimans in his baggage, which were all still in the possession of customs officials back in Cuba. He likewise wrote of Erna's recent trip with friends through the Belgian countryside and of the Dublon family's many walks in the forests outside Brussels. "How is Peter doing?" Willi asked, inquiring after Lore's longtime friend. "Our children are going to school again since yesterday, April 1, after fourteen days of Easter vacation. School is very demanding of them and we had already believed that nowhere would it be more difficult than in Erfurt." Aside from some illnesses, said Willi, "all is quiet and peaceful here."[2]

That was not to last. The Germans swept into Belgium one month later. Shortly after the takeover, Nazi officials conducted a census of all Jews in Brussels, a record that revealed the presence of Willi, Erna, Lore, Eva, and Erich.

Members of the Dublon family on the deck of the *St. Louis*, May 22, 1939. Willi Dublon stands second from the left. Erna and Erich are on the railing to his right. Eva and Lore stand in front. (USHMM, courtesy of Peter S. Heiman)

Of the five, it seems that Erich fell victim to the Nazis first. He was fifty-one years of age on August 11, 1942, the date Nazi records place him on a train bound from the Mechelen transit camp to Auschwitz. Belgian Convoy 2 arrived at Auschwitz two days later, on August 13. Of the 999 Jews in the convoy, 481 went directly to be gassed, while 290 men and 228 women entered the Auschwitz main camp as slave laborers. Given his age, Erich might well have been killed upon arrival. Yet this was not the case. The Auschwitz Death Books record Erich Dublon as a camp laborer who passed away of "congenital heart failure" on September 3, 1942.

Erich was not the only Dublon to meet his end at Auschwitz. The Gestapo arrested Willi Dublon on December 23, 1943, and sent him to Mechelen. The Gestapo then captured Erna, Lore (age sixteen), and Eva (age ten) on January 8, 1944. Seven days later, on the fifteenth, the Dublon family joined 658 other Jews (sixty-two of them children) on one of the very last convoys to leave Mechelen.

Their train, Convoy 23, arrived at Auschwitz on January 17, 1944. Upon arrival, 419 of the deportees went immediately to the gas chambers. Willi, Erna, and Eva are likely to have been among this number. Lore, on the other hand, was selected for forced labor and went to the Golleschau subcamp where she eventually died. Only twelve people from Convoy 23 remained alive at the time of Auschwitz's liberation; none were Dublons.

Sarah and Scott had uncovered the deportation of the Dublons very early in their research. As has been previously noted, the cruel calculus inherent in Sarah and Scott's project dictated, ironically, that those passengers who died in the Holocaust were usually far more easy to document than the living. But the appearance of the Dublons on this paperwork only informed Sarah and Scott about the end of their lives and revealed to them nothing about the people themselves. It took the researchers' fortuitous encounter with Peter Heiman, a witness who had known the Dublons in the flesh and loved them, to fill in the details of who they were as human beings. Only once this was done—only after Peter Heiman bore witness to Sunday hikes, jovial correspondence, and fondly remembered kindergarten days—could the true, full weight of the loss of the Dublons finally be recorded.

13

Washington Heights Portrait

The Fortunate

While nearly all of the *St. Louis* refugees found themselves denied entry to Cuba in 1939, a small percentage were allowed to land: some twenty-two[1] who had posted the $500 bond required by Cuba's Decree 55 and who thus possessed fully valid refugee visas. During one of their many research forays into Washington Heights, Scott and Sarah interviewed one of these more fortunate travelers.

Meta Bonne was well into her nineties when Sarah and Scott first met her. Despite her advanced age, she was spry as she ushered the researchers into her apartment at 181st Street and Riverside Drive. Inside the apartment, Meta's many well-appointed rooms were decorated in a way that said much about their owner. Meta's furnishings were top quality, solid, and expensive, but not ostentatious. The entire space, like Meta herself, was perhaps best summed up by the phrase "understated elegance." West-facing windows commanded a sweeping view of the Hudson River and the New Jersey Palisades, with the George Washington Bridge just a bit to the south.

Sitting down at her dining room table, Meta gestured for Sarah and Scott to do likewise. Then she began to talk. "Mine is one of the happier stories of the *St. Louis*," she said. "I think there are not so many of these, at least not so many as there should be." Pointing to several photos of her grandchildren, she continued: "You see, I have been lucky. Very lucky. God has held my family in the palm of his hand. Every day I remember this. But I also remember

Meta Bonne and the Isner family en route to Cuba, May 1939. From left to right: three unidentified passengers, Bella Isner, Meta Bonne, Betty Isner, Ruth Isner, and Justin Isner. (USHMM)

that I was a coward when I left that ship in Havana. I did not have the courage to turn around and look into the faces of those I was leaving behind in limbo. All they saw of me was my back as I walked away, down the gangplank, to the launch that took me and my babies to shore and to safety from Hitler."[2]

Known by her Jewish name, Miriam, to her family and friends, Meta was born Meta Honlein in Nuremberg in 1905. Her family was made up of Orthodox Jews, and her father was a successful merchant. "We didn't feel anything that was coming," she said of the days before the Nazis. "We never could have imagined. We seemed—to ourselves, at least—as much German and as much Bavarian as anyone." In 1930, when she was twenty-five years old, Meta married Martin Bonne, a wealthy businessman in the fur trade. "We moved into an apartment in Nuremberg. And that's where we were, in July of '33, when all this really got started, this hatred."

In Nuremberg on the evening of July 20, 1933, several squads of storm troopers methodically broke into more than four hundred Jewish homes, beating the men and confiscating all cash and valuables. "So many were victimized," Meta recalled. "But God spared us, as he would again on more than one occasion, despite our foolishness. No one banged on our door that night. No one invaded our home. No one took what was ours. It could have been. We had many friends who were hurt and robbed. And even though we were not personally attacked, we decided we should probably leave Germany."

Looking back, she professed astonishment at how long it took—six years—for her and her husband to finally take action on their decision of 1933. "We dawdled. We procrastinated and debated. Where to go? What country? We were quite stupid, and we were very picky and fickle. Our lives were in the balance, but we hesitated and discussed." At first the Bonnes considered South America, where many German Jews had migrated. "I was studying Spanish for a month already when Martin changed his mind, saying South America was no good. Too different a culture." Then, for a while, they contemplated the Netherlands, but the Dutch Interior Ministry denied them permission to immigrate. ("Another blessing," says Meta, referencing the many thousands of Jews from the Netherlands who eventually wound up in death camps.)

During 1934 the couple visited Palestine, where Martin's brother lived on a small kibbutz. Over the course of several weeks, Martin came to realize that the rough pioneering lifestyle of the Zionists was not for him. ("We do not need businessmen here," his brother told him categorically. "We need people who can work with their hands.") Recalling her husband, Meta began to laugh. "He was a man of the city, of starched shirts, of paperwork. He could not turn a screw or plant a root. If he ever tried to grow potatoes, they would come up rocks. He could be more helpful out of the country [Palestine] than in it, and he knew that." But, she added, "can you believe that in 1934 we *voluntarily* left Palestine and returned to Germany? I thank God every day that he took time to look after such idiots as us."

Meta gave birth to the couple's first child, Beatrice, in 1934. Four years later, the Bonnes were still tarrying in Nuremberg, contemplating their various options for departure, when Kristallnacht instilled a long-overdue sense of urgency. Kristallnacht saw the destruction of Nuremberg synagogues and storm troopers rounded up and beat some 160 Jewish men, most of whom were sent to Dachau shortly thereafter. "But not my husband," said Meta. "Once again God smiled."

Two months after Kristallnacht, in the wake of more round-ups of Jewish men, Martin Bonne traveled to Cuba, where one of Meta's brothers had already been living for several years. Martin's plan was to stay in Havana until his family could join him, after which they would all immigrate to the United States. During February, one month after Martin's departure, Meta gave birth to Jacob. (Meta got herself through the last stages of painful labor by reciting a simple three-word mantra over and over again: "Get to Cuba. Get to Cuba.") Shortly thereafter, she bought three tickets for the *St. Louis.*

Like other passengers, Meta obtained Cuban landing certificates—three of the Benitez certificates—directly through the Hamburg-America Line. With no reason to doubt the veracity of this paperwork, Meta subsequently thought it redundant when Martin, who'd heard rumors about an impending crisis related to the Benitez documents, sent her yet another landing certificate for the family signed not by Benitez but, rather, by the Cuban secretaries of state and labor and secured with the payment of $1,500 in cash bonds.

Speaking to Sarah and Scott, Meta described the westward passage of the *St. Louis* as "joyous. . . . We feel now we get to freedom." She said she recalled holding her infant son Jacob at a birthday party for Beatrice, who turned five aboard ship, and she reminisced fondly about a glamorous costume ball where she had "a grand time of champagne and dancing." Meta likewise said she remembered few premonitions of impending disaster, although her husband did telegraph her when the ship was two days out from Havana, warning that there "might be trouble" of some kind on the ship's arrival in Cuba.

On the afternoon of Saturday, May 27, as the *St. Louis* sat at anchor in Havana and concerned passengers queued up to speak with Cuban immigration officials, an announcement over the ship's public address system summoned Meta to report to the main salon along with her children and luggage. "The Cubans looked at my papers, first the Benitez certificates, then the other. It did not take long before they handed everything back to me and told me I was free to leave the ship." As she walked down the gangway to the waiting launch—her baby in her arms, her small daughter walking ahead of her, and some sailors carrying her suitcases—Meta focused "not on the past, what was in back of me, but the future, what lay ahead. It was all I could do. I had no power to help those I was leaving behind."

The Bonne family spent only a few months in Cuba, moving on to New York City in December 1939. They established themselves in Washington Heights one year later.

Martin Bonne died in 1979. Today Meta lives alone, and remains active in her Washington Heights community. Meta is a sisterhood member of the Orthodox synagogue K'hal Adath Jershurun, and she frequently attends afternoon teas held in the Moriah Adult Center on Bennett Avenue, where the language of choice is German.

Though Meta and her husband and children escaped the horrors of the Holocaust, they had many close family members who perished. When asked about those lost, Meta shakes her head and waves her hand. She prefers to focus on happier stories. She is especially proud of her husband's family in Israel, whom she has visited several times.

Although Meta does her best to accommodate those who seek information about the *St. Louis,* it is plain that she does not feel comfortable reflecting on the voyage. Her son Jacob, who became a thoroughly Americanized "Jack" during his childhood in New York, has been trying unsuccessfully for years to get Meta to set her memories down on paper. But he doubts she ever will. Looking out her window toward the panoramic view of the Hudson River, Meta seems content to sum up her slice of the *St. Louis* story with just twelve succinct and accurate words: "We were fortunate. Extremely fortunate. That is all I really have to say."

14

Washington Heights Portrait
Exile in America

The woman is nearing ninety years of age, and her white-walled apartment is, like her, both compact and immaculate. A rear window of her conservatively appointed living room overlooks the rich green landscape of Inwood Hill Park, abutting both the Hudson and Harlem Rivers at the northernmost extreme of Washington Heights. The splendid vista belies the fact that both the window and those who look through it are actually in Manhattan. But she is unimpressed. "Don't be deceived by the pleasant view," she says to Sarah and Scott, waving in the direction of the trees. "When I sit in my chair by the window, this is not what I see, these pretty green things. I only see the faces of my family. I have been in this apartment more than fifty years, and every single night I have sat in that chair and gone over and over again in my mind the events of the past. I am filled with guilt. . . . In that chair I sit and worry over all the *whys, if onlys,* and *what ifs* of my life."[1]

The woman stands with her arms crossed in the archway that leads from the hall to the living room. "I once thought of how to make all the *whys* and *what ifs* disappear. Only now I know I'm too much of a coward to commit suicide." Then, somewhat ruefully, she adds: "My doctor is not so sure. He knows I can't sleep, but he still won't give me a prescription for sleeping pills."

Walking about her living room, she eyes her surroundings with a sad familiarity. She has made this place her home ever since 1949, four years after her liberation from Auschwitz. On a table sits the latest edition of *Aufbau* opened to the obituaries. An array of books in both German and English line the shelves of several bookcases. And a number of large paintings, most with biblical themes, help reflect the sun from the window, making the room seem colorful and bright. Seeing Scott take note of the few photographs scattered about the space, the woman says, "All the pictures are of my family who were with me on the *St. Louis;* all of them were killed. I surround myself with the dead. Their story is my story."

Old world and old school in both her manners and her bearing, she insists on serving her guests coffee and cookies. Then, sitting across the table and munching on one of the sweets, she sighs and begins her tale.

Ilse Marcus was born on June 23, 1914, in Breslau, Germany, to Berthold and Elfriede Meyer. She had one sibling, a brother Ernst, born in 1918. Although she was the only Jewish girl in her school of six hundred, Ilse experienced no anti-Semitism while growing up in the 1920s. "It could be found everywhere in the world," she says, "[but] who would have thought it could appear in Germany, of all civilized places, in the way it did?" The Jews of Breslau felt secure. Pogroms, said Ilse's father, were for Poland and Russia and other such barbaric lands, not the country of Schiller and Beethoven. For proof of his theory, the prosperous Berthold Meyer needed only look around his own neighborhood. Breslau boasted the third-largest Jewish community in Germany. It also served as home to the country's largest rabbinical seminary.

Things began to change in 1933. That spring Nazi brownshirts murdered a number of young Breslau Jews and organized a boycott of Jewish-owned businesses. "Unfortunately," says Ilse, "despite the boycott, our family hardware business continued to go quite well. Therefore, from an economic standpoint, there was no reason for us to leave Germany. Still, my mother thought we should go." Ilse remembers her parents engaged in heated discussions on this point, her father clinging to the pride he took in both his German national identity and his status as a member of the merchant class. "Emigration is for second-class citizens," he told his wife. "We are first-class Germans. We are staying put. What is going on will soon pass." Berthold mistook the rising tide of anti-Semitism for nothing more than a momentary wave, one he thought would surely subside just as rapidly as it had swelled.

On September 15, 1935, the Reichstag passed the infamous Nuremberg Laws, greatly restricting Jewish life in Germany. Three months later, twenty-one-year-old Ilse married Kurt Marcus, an economist, and the couple moved in with Ilse's parents and brother in an apartment above the Meyer family store. Over the course of the next three years, the city police enforced anti-Jewish regulations with increased fervor, and many of the town's Jewish merchants were eventually forced to liquidate their businesses. Still, somehow, the Meyer hardware concern held on.

Ilse and her family were sound asleep in their rooms above the store on the night of November 9–10, 1938—Kristallnacht. Peeking out through upstairs shutters, Ilse watched looters carry away the contents of her father's business. Elsewhere throughout Breslau, Nazi thugs ransacked Jewish stores and schools and torched the city's synagogues. Ilse remembers her father coming into her room, shouting, "There's a pogrom out there." He was in shock. He could not believe what was happening.

Soon after, on the morning of November 11, storm troopers came to the family's apartment and arrested the men. Ilse's father, brother, and husband were sent to Buchenwald. Ilse and her mother breathed a sigh of relief when the three finally returned home three long weeks later, their release contingent on a promise to leave Germany. Without delay, the family traveled to the American consulate in Berlin to make formal applications for visas. The waiting numbers they received were very high. Ilse's was 52,327. It was clear it would be some time before they could get into the United States. They decided to follow the example of Kurt Marcus's brother, who had gone to Havana as a stopping-off point to wait for his own very high U.S. quota number to come up. When the three Meyers and two Marcuses purchased their tickets for the *St. Louis,* they did so using the very last of their ready cash. All of the family's property and assets had by this time been seized by the state. The store, the apartment, a lifetime of work—everything was gone.

Of the voyage itself, Ilse says little. She remembers her husband's brother approaching the *St. Louis* in Havana harbor on a small boat he had rented, shouting and waving. She remembers

Jewish refugees from Breslau on the deck of the *St. Louis*, May 1939. Seated in front is Ernst Meyer, standing left to right are Kurt Marcus, Ilse Marcus, a friend from Breslau, Elfriede Meyer, and Berthold Meyer. (USHMM, courtesy of Ilse Marcus)

Ilse and Kurt Marcus on board the *St. Louis*, May 1939. (USHMM, courtesy of Ilse Marcus)

the short, unhappy cruise from Havana to Miami, and then the utter dejection that followed. As the ship sailed away from the coast of Florida, Ilse turned to Kurt and exclaimed, "Simple cruelty! . . . How could anyone send even a dog back to Germany under such conditions?" Today, so many decades later, she turns to her visitors and declares: "At that moment we met the cruel face of America."

They wound up in Brussels. A year later, as German forces approached the city, Ilse and her family found themselves stranded, with the men facing arrest as enemy aliens and internment in France. "What an irony," Ilse exclaims. "To the Belgians, we Jews were Germans." Ilse told her husband he should not report to the authorities as ordered. "Hide here," she said, "and at least then we'll stay together." Kurt, however, was simply too afraid of getting caught, as were Ilse's father and brother. "My mother and I, the women in the family, were the risk takers," she says. The men wound up at the St. Cyprien camp and eventually the Gurs internment camp, both in southern France. For a time the area in which the camps lay remained unoccupied by the Germans. For a time letters went back and forth between the men and women. Berthold would often ask for money. The letters from Berthold, Ernst, and Kurt stopped in mid-1942. German troops moved into southern France in November 1942.

During May 1942, after nearly two years of occupying Belgium, the Nazis issued a decree ordering all Jews in the country to adopt badges similar to those worn by Jews in other German-occupied lands. Ilse refused. "We will never put on a yellow star," she told her mother. Instead, she purchased false identity cards on the black market. She remembers that very soon after receiving her fraudulent ID she was ordered at random to produce the document for a Gestapo officer she happened to encounter on the street. Ilse had not as yet studied and mastered the details of her new persona. The officer grabbed her papers and shouted, "When were you born?" Ilse, risking everything, answered just as loudly, "Can't you read? It's right there on the card!" Perhaps startled by Ilse's unlikely response—no one ever dared speak back to the Gestapo—the officer let her go.

But the incident frightened Ilse. Soon thereafter she decided that she and her mother would have to go into hiding. It was around this time that Ilse gave some of her personal belongings and documents to a Belgian family (former neighbors) for safe-keeping. During subsequent months, separated but in touch, Ilse and her mother lived in two different safe houses run by members of the Belgian resistance. Ilse worked in a laundry by day and read quietly in a dark basement room by night. Walking to and from work with false papers in her purse and no star on her chest, she frequently saw Jews being rounded up off the streets and shoved onto trucks. Resistance comrades told her that these Jews were usually brought to a transit camp called Mechelen, halfway between Brussels and Antwerp. From there, rumor had it, they were transported to a camp in the east. No one ever returned.

Early in January 1944, for reasons unknown to Ilse, the family to whom she had previously entrusted some of her possessions revealed both her Jewish identity and her whereabouts to the authorities. Ilse still recalls the "transfiguring fear" she experienced when several Gestapo officers barged unexpectedly into the laundry and dragged her out. Later, sitting on a bench at the police station, she encountered her mother, who was sick with the flu, and newly released from the Jewish infirmary, and now, like Ilse herself, bound for Mechelen. Once at Mechelen, mother and daughter simply waited a few days for the inevitable: transport to the east. The Nazis deported Ilse Marcus and Elfriede Meyer to Auschwitz in Convoy 23, departing Mechelen on January 15, 1944. The two women spent the long hours of the journey clinging to each other in a frigid freight car.

Nazi documents reveal the following about Convoy 23. It carried 662 Jews, sixty-two of whom were children. The trip to Auschwitz took two days. Five of the passengers did not survive the journey. After selection at Auschwitz on January 17, some 140 men and ninety-eight women were admitted to the camp as prisoners, receiving numbers 172296–172435 and 74512–74609. The remaining 419 people, Ilse's mother among them, died in the gas chambers almost immediately after their arrival.

Ilse describes the fate of the convoy in more personal terms. When the train arrived at Auschwitz-Birkenau, guards brutally pulled the human cargo out of the cars, shouting orders and savagely beating those who did not comply immediately. First the men and women were separated into two separate lines. Then an SS officer conducted the "selection" on the women's line, directing most of the women, including Ilse's mother, toward the gas chambers. Ilse joined the minority of females selected for forced labor. Ilse and her mother said nothing as they parted. "We simply looked at each other. Our faces were like stones. There was no facial movement. Though other people were shouting to each other, I did not hear a word. I only heard the silence of my mother's face."

Following this, the grief-stricken Ilse slowly adapted to the grim protocol of Auschwitz days and nights. She rose at 4 A.M., stood for roll call, and ate a meager breakfast. Then, from 6 A.M. to 6 P.M., she went to work carrying stones from one side of a field to another.

What bothered her most was the freezing cold. "I could live without food. . . . As the stomach shrinks, it wards off the pain of starvation." But against the cold there was no natural protection. She envied those already sent to the gas chamber—"they had it behind them already." She remembers saying to a friend, a fellow prisoner, "Let the end come already. I don't know how it will come, but it will. Death is better than the status quo." During her long days of labor, Ilse caught glimpses of piled-up skeletons and whiffs of burning flesh. She also saw men, women, and children walking forlornly toward the gas chambers.

Ilse's spirits lifted slightly when she was relieved from work in the fields and assigned to the night shift at a nearby munitions factory, where guns were manufactured and the heads of grenades prepared for the German war effort. All these years later, Ilse still displays great pride explaining how she jimmied the timing devices on many of the grenades, adjusting them to blow up in the hands of German soldiers the moment their pins were pulled. Ilse and the other workers also removed vital screws from the firing mechanisms of several hundred Mauser rifles on the assembly line.

In connection with the latter effort, Ilse remembers the day when camp commandant Rudolf Höss walked into the women's showers to confront them on the subject of the faulty Mausers. "It was so humiliating," she recalls. "Not only were we completely naked, but we were completely skeletal." Höss smirked at the skeletons as he announced that a large collection of recently produced rifles had proved unusable. By way of retribution, Höss executed several workers—all of them Polish—right on the spot. Spared that fate, Ilse returned to work and continued her sabotage. She did not care about being caught, since she believed that the end was coming anyway. "What I did could not save my life in the end, but it could take the lives of Germans, and that made it worthwhile."

Ilse constantly thought to herself: "We, the enfeebled prisoners, are doing whatever we can to save our lives and hurt the Nazis. Where are the great powers of the world?" She remembers that at one point, after the arrival of Jewish deportees from Hungary, she heard rumors that the Americans might soon start bombing the Auschwitz gas chambers. For weeks afterward she waited anxiously for the welcome rain of munitions. But it never came. "We weren't even worth a bomb to the Americans."

Freedom for Ilse came not via Allied bombing but rather through the efforts of Soviet soldiers who overran the camp on January 27, 1945. She weighed only seventy pounds on the day of her liberation. She recalls very little of what followed, just being put on a transport to a refugee camp in the Netherlands and thinking, "I'll never be the same again." Ilse carried with her a knife from the camp—a large trench knife emblazoned with a swastika—to rely on in case anyone threatened her. "All the trust was gone out of me," she says. "Never since Auschwitz have I been able to fully trust anyone."

From the Netherlands, Ilse eventually wandered back to Belgium. Once there, she moved into a tiny one-room apartment, made some money working in the black market, and began the search for her husband, brother, and father. During her spare hours, Ilse stood at the Brussels train station watching to see if any of her family were among the passengers arriving regularly from the east. She assumed that if they survived, they would show up again in Brussels. Ilse at first hoped that her father and brother remained among the living, but she remembers knowing instinctively that her husband was dead. "My Kurt was very weak. He just did not have what it takes to survive. Everyone always watched out for Kurt." Ilse remembers that when the family left Breslau for Hamburg to sail on the *St. Louis*, Kurt's mother ran alongside the moving train shouting: "Protect Kurt! Protect Kurt!" Nearly sixty years later, Ilse turned to Scott in tears and said, "I wish I could have protected my Kurt."

After a few months of standing watch at the train station, Ilse became discouraged and gave up. It was difficult for her to see the other survivors joyously reuniting with their loved ones. Ultimately, inquiries to the International Red Cross revealed all there was to know. Ilse's father had died at Majdanek in Poland and her husband and brother at Auschwitz.[2]

Ilse recalls that her grief after the war was compounded by a strong strain of anger. She had anger, first of all, for her one-time homeland, Germany. But she also had anger for the United States. Though most Belgians hailed the Americans as liberators and heroes, Ilse realized there were "two faces to America. And most Europeans knew only the good face."

Nevertheless, amid the despair she experienced in postwar Brussels, she took the necessary steps for immigration to the United States. Kurt's brother (the same man she had last seen waving from a rowboat in Havana Harbor) now lived in New York City. And so America eventually became Ilse's "home maybe in a physical sense, but not my homeland." She would rather have gone to Israel "and endured all the hardships of living in that land." But after losing her entire immediate family, she desperately wanted to be near someone—*anyone*—whom she could call kin. "I chose my exile. I chose to go to America." But she insists that it is not truly her country and never will be. "The Statue of Liberty means nothing to me. When we were here on the *St. Louis,* pleading for deliverance from evil, she sent us away. Her tablet says 'Give me your huddled masses, yearning to breathe free.' We were not a mass. We were just a little over nine hundred on the *St. Louis.* And more than yearning to breathe free, we were yearning just *to breathe, to survive.* To send the *St. Louis* back to Hitler's Europe was a criminal act. It was the greatest cruelty."

Ilse never remarried. Now an old woman, she sits in the chair by her window confronting the ghosts with whom she lives, wrestling with the past, and wondering what she (or the world) could have done differently to save her loved ones. "I see my mother walking to the gas chambers," she says. "I see her legs moving slowly. But most of all I see her face, her silent face. If only I could have done something. . . . If only the doctors in the Brussels Jewish infirmary [would have] thought to say that my mother had a contagious disease and was just too ill to be brought to Mechelen. She could have survived. There were, after all, other Jews who survived the war in that hospital."

The *if onlys* and *what ifs* never relent. "Why were we so passive while on board the *St. Louis?*" she wonders out loud. "What would have happened if we had gone on a hunger strike? And then, if only our family business had not been so successful, I could have convinced my father to emigrate sooner. What if we had left Germany before 1939? We would have been on a ship other than the *St. Louis,* arriving safely in Havana or some other port. My mother and I should have been more forceful in this regard."

Aside from her family photos, Ilse has few other possessions to remind her of life in Europe and her struggles during the Holocaust. One that she keeps with her always (for she has no other choice) is a string of numbers, 74560—the tattoo placed on her arm at Auschwitz. In her apartment, over coffee and cookies, Ilse reaches out to show the digits. They are barely visible. She once attempted to have them removed, but their smudged and still-decipherable pentimento remains, not far from a pulsing blue vein. "To me," says Ilse, "the numbers are not faint; they are as clear as day. And I know them like I know my name. They *were* my name for over a year."

A few photographs, a faded tattoo. What else does Ilse keep from those dark, distant, but still terribly vivid days when she lost those she loved most? Only one more thing: a small collection of letters sent to her by Kurt after his deportation to France. Ilse stores the letters in a bedroom cabinet but has not read them since the day in 1946 when she learned of her husband's death. Ilse at first hesitated when Scott, during his first visit to her apartment, asked if he could see the correspondence. As they walked from the living room into the bedroom, Ilse said, "Who knows if the letters are still there? I have been robbed so many times." But when she opened the cabinet, the small pile of dusty correspondence sat waiting. Ilse randomly took one of the notes, written in 1940 from the St. Cyprien camp, and read a few lines. She then looked up at Scott and said, "You see, my Kurt was trying to allay my fears. He did not want me to worry." To show what she meant, she read aloud from Kurt's comforting missive: "My dearest Ilse, Here in the camps in France they serve wine instead of water." As she read, tears flowed down Ilse's face.

Ilse did not proceed beyond Kurt's opening sentence. She folded the letter back into its envelope and then restored it to the cabinet with the rest. "Now you know where these are," she said, closing the cabinet firmly. "They will stay here, unread, until the day I die. After that, if you still are interested, you can come and read them."

15

Sowing in Tears

At the same time that Sarah and Scott made great research inroads in the United States, they also pursued leads worldwide, most notably in Israel. While Michael Barak had constituted Sarah and Scott's first success in Israel, additional personalities, stories, and archival materials soon emerged from within the Jewish homeland.

Sde Eliyahu lies in the fertile Beit Shean Valley not far from, but still two hundred meters below, the Sea of Galilee. The kibbutz comprises a beautiful green slice of the world. Here at this special place, religious Orthodoxy is emphasized in all things of the spirit and organic orthodoxy in all things of the soil. Home to 750, Sde Eliyahu encompasses more than 2,800 acres on which are grown everything from dates and pomegranates to potatoes, spices, and herbs. Additional Sde Eliyahu industries include Biobee, an effort in nonchemical pest control using natural predators, a dairy, and even a fish hatchery.

The founding members of Sde Eliyahu, German Jews, came to what is now Israel in 1934. They arrived as part of the Youth Aliyah movement and fully subscribed to one of that movement's main tenets: only the kibbutz model for living could be counted on to correct the economic ills of traditional Diaspora society. The desire of these young people was twofold: to return to Israel from the outside world and to return to life on the land. After four years of agricultural training at a camp near Jerusalem, the small group of settlers (supplemented by several more recent arrivals from Germany) built a rough "tower and stockade" settlement

more than one hundred miles north of Jerusalem. Thus Sde Eliyahu was launched.

When the tower and stockade went up, the lands at Sde Eliyahu were harsh, impoverished, and unusable, nothing more
than a mosquito-ridden swamp demanding the back-breaking
work of reclamation.[1] Today, not only the swamp but also the
primitive tower and stockade are long gone. In place of the first
simple, bare-bones structures modern Sde Eliyahu boasts numerous comfortable buildings and amenities. Residents share meals
in a large, well-lit dining hall. Medical care, education, and housing are supplied communally according to need. A relatively
high percentage of the workforce pursues advanced studies. And
the weekly "general meeting" constitutes the supreme authority
on the kibbutz, a successful exercise in direct democracy.

At Sde Eliyahu the imperative for an agrarian lifestyle remains one of the driving forces at the heart of the Zionist idea.
Close to seventy years after its founding, the once-barren land of
the kibbutz has been completely transformed by two generations
of sweat. It now includes members from Italy, France, the United
States, and many other countries.

It was to this place—at once idyllic and challenging—that
Sarah and Scott came in March 2000. But what they wanted at
Sde Eliyahu was not a taste of kibbutz living; nor was it a chance
to view Beit Shean's many splashes of historically significant,
verdantly beautiful landscape. What Sarah and Scott sought at
Sde Eliyahu were remnants of the past.

Sarah and Scott's journey to Sde Eliyahu had in fact begun close
to a year before. During April 1999, fifty-three-year-old Yehudit
Silber, a proud, second-generation member of the kibbutz, had
unearthed treasure while doing her Passover cleaning. The treasure was in the form of an old cardboard box forgotten and abandoned in the corner of the attic where Yehudit's mother had
stored it years before. The box held a large collection of old letters written in German. The letters—sent before and during
World War II to Yehudit's mother and father, two founders of Sde
Eliyahu—came from Adolf Gruenthal, her father's uncle.

Yehudit had grown up with the vague understanding that
Adolf Gruenthal, his wife, and two sons (along with a second
uncle, Walter, and his wife and their two daughters) had all

The extended Gruenthal family in Gleiwitz, Germany, before the voyage of the *St. Louis*. Adolf is on the far right. (USHMM, courtesy of Yehudit Silber)

perished in the Nazi death camps. Beyond these facts, however, she had been given no details. Indeed, she had assumed there were none to give, that anonymity had swallowed her relatives' unique experiences reducing them to the status of mere abstractions. But the relics retrieved from Yehudit's attic did much to fill in the details of her lost relatives' stories.

Astonishingly to Yehudit, these letters from the past indicated that the Gruenthals had actually left Germany in 1939, sailing to Cuba on the *St. Louis* only to be turned back. This revelation was fresh on Yehudit's mind one month later when she noticed an article in the Israeli daily *Ma'ariv* about the *St. Louis* and a special exhibition being mounted at the United States Holocaust Memorial Museum in Washington, D.C. Investigating further on the Museum's website, Yehudit learned of Sarah and Scott's effort to trace the fates of the ship's passengers. She then made contact, inviting the two researchers to the kibbutz, where she offered to show them her extensive cache of family correspondence.

Boarding a bus in Jerusalem's central station, Sarah and Scott traveled two hours north. The bus descended from the Jerusalem hills toward the Dead Sea before veering on through the Jordan

Valley. Passing the ancient city of Jericho, the bus then rolled further on to Beit Shean, with its extensive excavation sites where
twenty-eight layers of civilization have been uncovered over the
course of several decades. Finally, in the middle of what appeared
to be nowhere, Scott and Sarah arrived at Sde Eliyahu junction.
Here a man they had never met before—a gentleman who turned
out to be Yehudit's husband, Avraham Silber—escorted them to
his van for the last leg of the journey. Out the van windows to
the left they could see Israel's Mount Gilboa and to the right the
Gilead Mountains of Jordan above the rich green fields of the
kibbutz.

Greeting them at Sde Eliyahu, Yehudit proved to be a robust
and generally cheerful woman. She brought Sarah and Scott to
lunch at Sde Eliyahu's large dining hall and then energetically
escorted them on a walking tour through the kibbutz's school,
gardens, meeting hall, and synagogue. Following this, Yehudit
walked Sarah and Scott back to her home. Here her previously
ebullient mood became more somber. She described what it was
like to live and grow up in Israel knowing that so many other relatives, lost in the Holocaust, would never be able to share that
privilege, that joy. Yehudit brought out family photo albums containing images of those who perished. These included portraits
of the Gruenthals, school photos, and snapshots from Berlin
where the Gruenthals had evidently led an affluent urban existence before the rise of the Nazis.

Yehudit read aloud in Hebrew (already translated from the
original German) from Adolf Gruenthal's letters. "At this moment," the desperate man had written from the *St. Louis* in Havana harbor on May 28, 1939, "we are anxiously waiting to hear
from the Cuban government. We are hearing now all types of
outrageous rumors from Cuba. Now even here they are refusing
to admit Jews. The situation is very sad."[2] Later, from somewhere in the middle of the Atlantic, he wrote: "We experienced
very emotional days. Stormy. I suspect that there will be more
like these ahead of us. . . . We hope somebody, somewhere will
take us in. Not knowing where we are heading is a terrible fate."[3]
From the Netherlands on June 25, Mr. Gruenthal reported: "We
have arrived in Rotterdam, and [have been] placed in Heyplaat
[an internment center]. We have received permission to stay in
Holland for one year. We are concerned that we might not be able

to stay more than this. I fear that there will be the same deception as in Cuba."[4]

Reading through other family letters and diary entries, Yehudit deduced that in April 1940 both Gruenthal families were interned at the Westerbork refugee camp. Life there was filled with anxiety for the adults, but the four Gruenthal children flourished. The young cousins—Lutz (11), Horst Martin (9), Ruthild (12), and Sibyll (9)—all joined the Zionist pioneer group Machar (Tomorrow) and became members of the small training kibbutz organized within the camp. The children wore blue-and-white Zionist uniforms and worked a plot of land in preparation for the agricultural life to be found in Palestine. The children also participated in *sichot* (discussions) of Zionism, danced the hora, and sang *HaTikva* ("The Hope"), the future national anthem of the State of Israel.

Adolf Gruenthal's letters stopped in mid-1942, shortly after the German authorities, who had controlled the Netherlands since 1940, seized direct authority over the Westerbork camp. Reports from the children ceased a year later.

Sarah and Scott, with their extensive contacts and resources at the Museum, found themselves sadly able to offer Yehudit a few details about the abyss into which her family members had fallen.

Dutch and German documents indicated that Adolf and his wife, Bertha, as well as Adolf's brother Walter and sister-in-law Margarethe and their two girls, Ruthild and Sibyll, were deported in September 1944 to the Theresienstadt ghetto near Prague and later to Auschwitz. Bertha, Margarethe, and Sibyll's last-known location was Auschwitz, where most likely they perished in the gas chambers. Adolf, on the other hand, was interned at Auschwitz III, a part of the Buna Monowitz forced-labor complex, in October 1944. From there, on an unknown date, he was transferred to the Golleschau subcamp, his last traceable location. Meanwhile, with regard to Walter and his daughter Ruthild, records indicated their final destination was somewhere in "Middle Europe."

Sarah and Scott had no official documentation to share with Yehudit concerning Adolf's sons Lutz and Horst Martin. However, they had been in touch with another family member (a cousin of whom Yehudit was only vaguely aware) who lived in the Israeli seaside town of Netanya. Eva Willenz wrote of the two

Sibyll and Ruthild Gruenthal in the Westerbork transit camp during World War II. (USHMM, courtesy of Yehudit Silber)

boys: "They [Lutz and Horst Martin] had a[n immigration] certificate for Palestine—but since they had come to visit and observed
how hard our life was here in those days, they didn't want to
come here. They were hoping for something better [in Europe].
Alas—they never achieved that, but were deported to Bergen-
Belsen [and]—so far as I know—perished there."[5]

When Sarah and Scott read this account to Yehudit, she observed, "How ironic, young Lutz and Horst, after being rejected
by Cuba and the United States, were given the rare chance to
make it to Palestine and did not avail themselves of the opportunity." Certificates for immigration to Palestine were rare during
the time the Gruenthal boys found themselves given that option.
Lutz and Horst Martin had been among a select few. As she
spoke, Yehudit gazed out at the flowering kibbutz gardens. "I
want to say to Lutz and Horst, 'sure, things were harsh here, but
look at the fruits of our labor.'" She then quoted Psalm 20: "'He
who sows in tears will reap in joy.' Lutz and Horst Martin Gruenthal ended their lives just sowing tears."[6]

After this exchange, Yehudit began to walk with Sarah and
Scott toward the home of her eighty-three-year-old mother, Ruth
Kobliner, who was off enjoying the day on her bicycle. Later, over
tea and cookies Ruth described (in Hebrew laced with a thick
German accent) how she had fled Nazi Germany for Palestine
in 1936. She then helped found the kibbutz in 1938, and since
that time she has dedicated her life to renewing the land of Sde
Eliyahu.

Comfortably settled into her adopted home, Ruth felt that
Europe and the events of World War II seemed very far away.
Unlike her daughter, she did not choose to spend much time
thinking about the Holocaust, despite having been much closer
to it in time and space. She had lived in Berlin before migrating
to Palestine. Adolf and Walter Gruenthal were her in-laws, her
husband's uncles. It was Ruth and her husband who received
Adolf's letters, first from the *St. Louis* and then from the Netherlands. All these years she had known about those relatives, including the fact that they were on the *St. Louis*, but she had never
related their story to her daughter. "Look," said Ruth, "we were
here to build. We were too busy draining swamps to cry. We
could not look back. What else could we do?" She then intoned

the Zionist-pioneering motto: "We came to this land to build, and be rebuilt by it," adding, "to rebuild, we had to *separate* [from Europe]."[7]

Mother and daughter had each been marked in different ways by the fates that befell their relatives from the *St. Louis.* Both had made a good and happy life on the kibbutz, but Ruth's turning away from the past stood in sharp contrast to Yehudit's desire to reconnect. After saying goodbye to Ruth, Sarah and Scott walked with Yehudit back to her house. As the three of them walked, the sun set over Mount Gilboa. Later on, just as Sarah and Scott prepared to leave, Yehudit entrusted her letters and photographs to them. "Don't forget us here on the kibbutz," she told them by way of farewell, "and don't forget what happened to my relatives."

The documentation of Yehudit's eight relatives from the *St. Louis* combined with still more stories discovered by Sarah and Scott in the twelve months prior to their Sde Eliyahu visit brought the researchers' unaccounted-for list down into the low teens.

16

States of Insecurity

On the day after the visit to Sde Eliyahu, Scott visited a cramped office in Jerusalem to search for two other *St. Louis* passengers—or at least their stories.

The office Scott visited was as tiny as it was disheveled. The Jewish Agency's Missing Persons Bureau had, in fact, seen better days. As the Holocaust receded further in time, and the number of institutions with sophisticated survivor and victim databases grew, the low tech Missing Persons Bureau—once a first stop for many survivors and relatives looking for loved ones who might have immigrated to Palestine—no longer seemed all that relevant or necessary. Indeed, many of the bureau's services had been cut by the time Scott visited, and the skeleton staff was operating on a shoe-string budget.

In a sign on the door, the bureau announced itself in three languages. In addition to the standard Hebrew and English, Scott noted a Russian translation. As Scott entered the tight space, he found himself at the back of a line of Soviet Jews, recent immigrants in search of family members who they hoped or believed had settled in Israel following the war. Some carried documents or photos to help identify those they were looking for. Others had only their memories or the memories of aged parents left behind in the former Soviet Union. As Scott awaited his turn at the desk, he saw some of the refugees receive the joyous news that they could soon be reunited with loved ones alive in Israel. But he also witnessed the majority have their hopes dashed, informed that their relatives most likely did not survive the Holocaust or survived and then had died in Israel years before.

This later scenario, Scott knew already from his previous correspondence with the bureau, was the case with the subjects of his quest today: Richard and Betty Blum, natives of Poland and passengers on the *St. Louis.*

Richard Blum was born on August 28, 1886, in Schrimm (also spelled Srem), Poland, a small town some twenty-five miles from Poznan and a place where only about a hundred Jews lived in the prewar years. Betty Blum (nee Simon) was born on January 20, 1891, in Zydowo, Poland. A tailor of women's clothing, Richard migrated at some point with Betty to Berlin, although as Polish Jewish refugees it proved impossible for them to obtain German citizenship. During December 1938, a month after Kristallnacht, the Blums registered for visas at the U.S. consulate in Berlin, receiving waiting numbers 9,970 and 9,971 on the Polish quota. (The Polish quota was about six thousand, considerably smaller than the German one.) The Blums then booked passage on the *St. Louis,* planning, like so many others, to make Cuba their home until their turn came for entry into the United States. After the *St. Louis* returned to Europe, the Blums found themselves in Belgium.

More than fifty years later, Sarah and Scott's initial search for documentation concerning the fates of the Blums turned up frustratingly little. One piece of paper placed Betty Blum at the French internment camp Gurs in 1940 and noted her release after several months. One other item indicated that the Blums were among refugees receiving aid.[1]

When a couple of false leads failed to pan out, Sarah and Scott, reaching in some desperation for a final resource, wrote to the Missing Persons Bureau. Not expecting much to come of their request—indeed, having no firm evidence that the Blums ever made aliyah to Israel—the two researchers were delighted, a few weeks later, to get a response. The note from Bureau Chief Batya Unterschatz was handwritten on letterhead of the Jewish Agency's Finance Bureau, with the words "Finance Bureau" crossed out. It appeared that the Missing Persons Bureau no longer even had its own letterhead. It did, however, still have vital informational resources not duplicated anywhere else in the world, and now Batya provided the details Sarah and Scott had been looking for: "Blum Richard, *Reuven ben Abraham* [Reuven

Richard and Betty Blum on board the *St. Louis* en route to Cuba, May 14, 1939.
(USHMM, courtesy of Richard Blum)

son of Abraham], b 28.8.86, came to Palestine in October 1947
and died in Haifa in October 1979. His wife Betty, *Betty bat Israel*
[Betty daughter of Israel], b. 1891, died in July 1975. I do not
know if they had children in Israel."[2]

Even though Batya indicated she did not know whether or
not the Blums had children, Sarah and Scott wrote her asking
how this might be verified. Batya replied by e-mail: "You can
find out more on the Blums, but you will have to come to Israel to
do it; it will require 'schlepping,' lots of leg work. . . . Your first
stop has to always be at the Bureau. That's where all searches
begin."[3]

Thus Scott began the second phase of the search two years
later at the bureau. Once Scott reached the head of the line, he
learned that the woman he had seen dealing so well with the
new émigrés—speaking to them in an easy mix of Hebrew, Yiddish, and Russian—was the same Batya (an émigré herself, from
Latvia) with whom he and Sarah had been corresponding. As
she walked Scott to her desk behind the counter, Batya moved
slowly and complained that her eyes were hurting her. The vast
majority of her daily searching, she explained to Scott, was conducted via one antiquated microfilm reader on which she routinely had to search through hundreds of barely legible immigration lists supplied by the Israeli Interior Ministry. Batya told Scott
that more modern equipment would be a nice luxury but was
not essential. "Through this one lousy machine I have found
thousands of refugees being searched for, reuniting them with
their families. . . . I found them, safe and sound, or a record of
them, in Israel. . . . Reuniting Jewish refugees in Israel is like putting back the pieces from a rupture."[4]

Leaning over her microfilm as Scott watched, Batya confirmed that the Blums came to Palestine without children. Nor
was there any record of Betty giving birth later—an unlikely
prospect in any event, since Betty would have been well into her
fifties at the time of her arrival in the Middle East. For his part,
Scott knew that the Blums had traveled without children on the
St. Louis. Given all this, it seemed a reasonably safe conclusion
that the Blums had no living descendants and that if Scott
wanted to learn of their lives after the *St. Louis* he would have to
rely on the memories and anecdotes of old friends and neighbors, provided these could be found.

Batya had an address—number 14 on HaHorev Street in Haifa—that appeared on both Richard and Betty's death certificates. "Go talk to the neighbors," she counseled Scott. "The Blums died less than thirty years ago; some of the neighbors have to be the same. In Israel, sometimes neighbors know more than children. That's your best bet. . . . If that fails, go to the Haifa Burial Society [Hevra Kadisha]. The society will be able to say who pays for the care of the graves. And in turn, these people might know the Blums' stories."

Scott took the bus to Haifa that same day. As he approached the sprawling city on the hills just above the Mediterranean, it made sense to him that the Blums—who had spent two decades in Berlin after emigrating from Poland—would settle here. By and large, immigrants from Germany built Haifa. The German Jewish refugee community made its mark on the city even before the Holocaust, giving it a distinctive character and making it a welcome destination for survivors from Germany after the war. Here, in this city by the sea, thousands of Holocaust survivors had stepped onto the soil of Palestine for the first time.

Once off the bus, Scott bought a local map and quickly located the Blums' street. Conveniently, it was not far from the bus station, just a bit farther down the hill, closer to the port in a modest neighborhood that seemed an old immigrant stronghold. Number 14 HaHorev, however, turned out to be not an apartment building or a single family home but a nursing home. Moreover, it was a nursing home that had changed hands since the 1970s, when the Blums had ended their days there. No records remained and the staff was completely different. Here at 14 HaHorev there was no memory of the couple who held for Scott such deep interest.

Next, Scott proceeded to Batya's alternative suggestion, the Hevra Kadisha. This burial society is located in the city center at 63 Herzl Boulevard. The three-story building houses the various offices of the Haifa Rabbinate: a rabbinical court, a birth records and registration center, a marriage and divorce records center, and the Hevra Kadisha.

Just one staffer attended the Hevra Kadisha office. He was an elderly gentleman with a long white beard, clad in ultra-orthodox black garb. Here the lingua franca was Yiddish, and at first the man seemed chagrined by the request Scott mumbled in

a halting mixture of Yiddish and Hebrew spiced with a pronounced New York accent. Unlike most other visitors to this office, Scott's intention was not to locate tombstones and pay respects. Rather, he was interested in research. "Research?!" the
attendant exclaimed, before turning to his books of records, his
rosters of the dead. Explaining his business further, Scott mentioned that these people, the Blums, were childless. Thus he was
interested in speaking to whoever was paying for the care of
their grave. After spending a few minutes with the books, however, the old record keeper told Scott he was wrong. In fact, the
Blums had a son, Hanan Blum, who was alive in Israel. The old
man jotted down an address—on Kibbutz Ein Gev—and a phone
number. Then he printed out copies of the Blums' burial certificates for Scott to take away with him.

That evening, Scott called Hanan Blum at the kibbutz, identified himself, and asked if Hanan's parents were Richard and
Betty Blum of the *St. Louis*. At first, Hanan greeted this inquiry
with silence. Then, hesitatingly, he said "yes." An even longer
silence followed after Scott explained the nature of his mission.
Then, finally, Hanan announced that, at age eighty-six, this was
an emotional moment for him because it had been years since he
last talked of the Holocaust with anyone. He added that he
wanted to put the past behind him—that was, his parents' past.
The Holocaust, he insisted, was not even really a part of his own
personal history. He had seen the writing on the wall and, as a
young man, fled Germany in 1936 on what he termed "the onward march to Palestine." He now considered his first language
to be Hebrew, not German, the language of the country where he
had been born. He was among the pioneering founders of Kibbutz Ein Gev, living for the first few years in a hut, always with a
vision and plans of building. His parents, in contrast, had their
own hopes for a better life in Germany, the "promised land" to
which they came from Poland. By 1939, however, Richard and
Betty Blum were finished with Germany and willing to book
passage anywhere, on the first ship available. As fate decreed,
this would be the *St. Louis*.

In his conversation, Hanan skipped over the details of his
parents' experiences during the war and instead focused on
more contemporary topics—specifically, the position of his kibbutz, which lay just below the Golan Heights on the eastern side

of the Sea of Galilee. "For nineteen years," said Hanan, "we were shelled by the Syrians from atop the Golan Heights and lived with the scourge of terrorism, and now the government wants to take away our security by giving the Golan back, a plan that would dislodge Jews from their homes. So you see, at this juncture in history, as they are talking about giving back our territory and returning us to a state of insecurity, it is hard for me to think about my parents' insecurity during the Holocaust." Also, Hanan told Scott, he was now slightly deaf and found it difficult to talk over the phone. "Write me, and I'll write you back. Or better yet, come visit me on the kibbutz."[5]

Another year would pass before Scott had the opportunity to take Hanan up on his invitation. It was a fine spring morning in June 2001 when the bus from Tiberias dropped Scott off at the entrance to Ein Gev. As he approached the gates of the kibbutz, Scott was immediately greeted by an older member of the commune who wasted no time in pointing to the top of the nearby Golan Heights, noting that this was the site where Syrian cannon were positioned in the years between 1948 and 1967. "These cannon were not just sitting there for their health," the man declared. "They were shelling Ein Gev." Only after making his point about the Heights did he ask Scott's business and who he was looking for.

"Ah, Hanan Blum," he responded, once Scott had uttered the name, "one of our founders. What do you want with Hanan?" When Scott said he wanted to speak with Hanan about the Holocaust, his greeter countered, "Well, why just him? Half the people on this settlement are survivors." He then began to recite a long litany of names and where they were during the war. After Scott interrupted, briefly explaining details of the *St. Louis,* the man showed clear signs of not understanding what he was talking about. Nevertheless, he pointed out Hanan's distant cabin, a small place overlooking the Sea of Galilee draped with a banner that read "The People Are with the Golan."

Believing himself now to be late for his 9 A.M. appointment with Hanan, Scott walked briskly toward the little dwelling and knocked. He walked in to find an elderly woman. "Shalom," she said. "I am Batya Blum. You probably came here by bus from Tiberias, correct?" When Scott nodded yes, she said, "You are lucky you can travel here by land. When the Arabs used to riot during the early days of the kibbutz, we could only access Ein Gev by boat."

Reminding Batya that he was from the United States Holocaust Memorial Museum in Washington, D.C., Scott then inquired as to her husband's whereabouts. The word *Holocaust,* however, set her conversation off in another direction. Batya told Scott that she left Vienna on March 14, 1938, the day after the German annexation of Austria, and made her way to Palestine. She then began to cry and said that she never saw her parents again; they were deported to Auschwitz. It was only after she had composed herself that she said, decisively: "You are here for Hanan. Well, Hanan is in Tiberias getting his eyes checked. The kibbutz brought all the old people to the eye doctor. He should be returning in about an hour."

Batya served Scott a cup of coffee and entertained him with stories about the early days of the kibbutz until Hanan arrived. Hearty, vigorous, but apparently hesitant to speak of his parents or the *St. Louis,* Hanan instead reminisced about his own experiences during the early years of Nazi rule. He was in the Zionist Techelet Lavan (Blue and White) youth movement in Berlin and then went with the HeHalutz (Pioneer) to Breslau to organize for making aliyah. He continued by describing his aliyah to Israel in 1936 and his parents' opposition to his emigration.

"Ein Gev was isolated during the 1948 War of Independence," he told Scott. Pointing out his front window to the Sea of Galilee he exclaimed, "You see all the way to the other side? That's Tiberias. That was the closest Jewish settlement in 1948." Then, turning around, he pointed out his back window. "You see the Golan Heights? From 1948 through 1967 we suffered from severe Syrian air and artillery attacks from atop these mountains. Frequent attacks—constant exposure. My three children were brought up in bomb shelters, and now there's talk about giving the Golan back to Syria."

Only after relaying all this did Hanan finally get to the story that Scott had come so far to hear, the story of Richard and Betty Blum.

Though Hanan was in Palestine by 1939, his parents had decided to immigrate to America because Richard Blum had a brother there. Thus, they booked passage on the *St. Louis.* After the return of the ship to Europe, Hanan corresponded with his parents in Belgium. Then, following the German invasion of western Europe in May 1940, the letters stopped. After a while, Hanan contacted the JDC, asking them to locate his parents. He received a response in early 1941. Expecting the worst, he was surprised to read that his parents were alive and living in Nice, France, where they had fled in mid-1940 after the German invasion of Belgium.

Following Mussolini's occupation of French territory in November 1942, Nice came under Italian jurisdiction. This regime was less severe for Jews than German occupation. Nevertheless, Richard and Betty went into hiding in Nice with a family that Hanan remembered his parents identifying only as "the Brauns." Even while in hiding, Richard was able to continue his work as a tailor and interacted with many people in Nice who were sympathetic to Jews.

The situation became more perilous for Richard and Betty after German troops invaded the Italian-occupied zone around Nice on September 8, 1943. Soon special SS units rolled into town to search for Jews. Richard ceased work. House raids became a daily occurrence. Several homes right on the Brauns' street were ransacked. Within five months, five thousand Jews were caught and deported. Somewhat miraculously, the Brauns' home never became the target of a raid. Richard and Betty lived out the rest of the war in hiding, never leaving the Brauns' house. "The Brauns must have been wonderful people," sighed Hanan. "I have two regrets: that we did not keep up with them after my parents left Europe and that we never sought to have them recognized as rescuers, as 'Righteous Among the Nations' at Yad Vashem."

After the war ended, Richard and Betty Blum abandoned their hopes of migrating to the United States. Though not imbued with the same Zionist spirit as Hanan, they decided that they should be near their son. It took two years for them to get their immigration certificates from the British, but they were able to come to Palestine—soon to be Israel—in 1947. They arrived in Haifa during Arab riots in the city and, despite the climate in that town, decided to settle there. The JDC helped them find a modest apartment with a bathroom shared by several families. In 1950, after receiving restitution money from Germany, they were able to buy a nicer apartment. And Richard Blum, as he had all along from Poland to Berlin to Nice, continued his professional life as a tailor.

Hanan Blum expressed surprise when Scott presented him with Red Cross documentation showing that his mother had been interned in Gurs from May 15, 1940, through August 15, 1940. "I had no idea," he said. "You see, my parents did not discuss their experiences. All I know about my parents during the Holocaust was from the letters they wrote me. [Letters not kept by Hanan.] Survivors in Israel did not talk in those years, and their children did not ask questions." Then, again pointing to the Golan Heights, Hanan said simply, "Hopefully we can keep these hills, so I won't have to flee all over again. That's not what I or my parents came to this land for."[6]

The case of Richard and Betty Blum had been solved, but never really closed. Through the detective work of the Missing Persons Bureau, the records of the Haifa Burial Society, and the testimony of Hanan, Sarah and Scott could with certainty mark the Blums as survivors. Hanan, however, because he did not know or, more likely, did not want to look back, could not provide Sarah and Scott with as much information as they would have liked. What was missing for them were more of the wartime experiences of Richard and Betty Blum—in their *own voices.*

This was to change three years later on a winter day when an elderly gentleman in Haifa was surfing the internet. On February 24, 2003, this individual sent the following e-mail message to Scott: "I found articles about the *St Louis* over the internet—on the USHMM website. I am the son of Richard and Betty Blum, signed, Seev Blum."[7]

Scott was bewildered. Who was *Seev* Blum? He only knew a *Hanan* Blum. Neither the Missing Persons Bureau nor the Haifa Burial Society had any records of a Seev Blum. And more significantly, Hanan never mentioned him. "*Why* Hanan never mentioned me," Seev was eventually to tell Scott, "I have no idea. Though now that we are older and less mobile Hanan and I do not see each other much, given the journey between Haifa on the Mediterranean and Kibbutz Ein Gev on the Golan Heights."

Scott and Seev exchanged e-mails for about a year and then in January 2005, Scott traveled to Israel and met with Seev, who was living in a rather upscale senior residence in Haifa. Seev was waiting for Scott in the lobby, where the two sat and had a cup of coffee. If there had been any residual doubts as to whom Seev really was, Scott immediately could see the resemblance between him and Hanan.

Seev's first words to Scott were the following: "I, born Siegfried Blum, now Seev Blum, came to Palestine in 1934, and was at first one of the founders of Kibbutz Ha-Miphne, and later of Kibbutz Dalia. My older brother Hans, now Hanan, as you know, came to Palestine in 1936 and was a member of Kibbutz Ein Gev, where he lives today." As with his brother Hanan, Seev provided great detail—infused with Zionist ideology and much enthusiasm—about his life as a kibbutz pioneer in Palestine during the 1930s and into the war years. And also like Hanan, Seev's recollection of what was happening in Europe—"back there"—as he was on the kibbutz was sparse.

At first Scott believed that Seev would not be able to add much to Hanan's account as the elderly gentleman began to relay the following basic facts about his parents' sojourns (some of which overlapped with the information Hanan provided; some of it different): "When my parents disembarked in Belgium they were sent to Brussels where the Jewish Committee received them, and settled them in a hotel, and later found a room for them with some Belgian family. My father had some business friends in Paris, from whom he bought fabrics for his business, and they helped my parents (two days before the German entered Brussels) to fly to Paris. They were, however, arrested by the French authorities and sent to the camp in Gurs."

"*They?*" asked Scott. "A Gurs document only exists for your mother." Seev explained: "My father's name does not appear on any document because, as my mother told me, the staff of the camp took my father to the hospital every time an inspection took place. Later my parents were able to leave the camp and went to Nice, where they stayed to the end of the war." Seev then continued with the last chapter of his parents' life story: "They came on a regular ship from Marseille to Haifa, and lived together with my family in a small flat in Haifa. Later the Jewish Agency found a flat for them together with another family, at Jaffa Street in Haifa. When they received their first restitution payments from the German government they bought a small flat in Mount Carmel neighborhood. Years later they went to the home for the elderly (on HaHorev Street) where they lived until the end of their days."

By this point Scott discerned a number of differences present in Hanan's and Seev's accounts of their parents' wartime sojourns. Seev, unlike Hanan, was aware of the Gurs internment. On the other hand, Seev said he had never heard from his parents that they were in hiding in Nice, as Hanan described. "There was mention of their taking on assumed identities," recalled Seev, "but never that they were rescued." Scott then brought up the name "Braun," the family name of the non-Jewish rescuers, according to Hanan. Indeed, Seev recognized the name Braun, but not as a family of non-Jewish rescuers, but rather of *Jewish* relatives of his father that lived in Hamburg before the war. "The Brauns had a big import and export business, dealing mainly in grain," Seev added. "There were two brothers, Bruno and Max. Bruno went to Amsterdam and opened a business there, and Max went to San Francisco where he similarly opened a business. Our families were close. . . . Could Hanan have confused the names," mused Seev, "or was it just coincidence as Braun is a fairly common name—who knows? The bottom line is that my parents mentioned nothing to me about being in hiding."

Then Seev concluded his parents' story with the following sentence: "Look . . . I don't know all the facts—neither does Hanan. We both left Germany at a young age against our parents' will, and so after that we were not interested in family affairs, or in the affairs of the 'old country.' Also, when my parents at last came to Palestine, they *absolutely* did not want—or were not able—to speak of what they went through during the war. *They did not speak of it.*"

How then, Scott asked, was Seev able to reconstruct his parents' story if they did not talk? The answer was literally handed to Scott by Seev. It was a pile of letters that his parents had written before, during, and immediately after the war years detailing their experiences. In the written word the Blums could express what they could not bear to say. Revealed in the letter on the top of the pile, written in Berlin April 6, 1939, was the first Seev heard that his parents would be sailing to Cuba: "We have managed to get a visa for Cuba with the help of a friendly gentleman. If everything goes well, i.e. after we have completed all the formalities here, we will arrive there, God willing, on the twenty-seventh of May. Then, we will have to wait in Cuba until we can manage to get into the U.S. and hope that it will go faster from there on. It is not the way we thought it would be and our hope to see you children again has been shattered. If we knew that we could get into Palestine, we would have preferred that, of course."[8]

May 1939 came and went and Seev assumed that his parents were—as they had described—safely in Cuba waiting for their U.S. quota number to be called. Later that June, however, Seev received a letter from his parents postmarked not Havana—but Brussels—an indicator that something had gone terribly wrong. On July 19, 1939, Betty Blum wrote the following from Brussels to her son Seev:

> For the past two days we have been back on land, after five weeks of being on this adventurous ship. Like the other 900 passengers, we have prepared everything legally; the thugs, however, did not let us land. . . . We nearly fell back into the Nazis' clutches again—but we wouldn't have let that happen. In the last moment we received the message that England, France, Holland, and Belgium would give us shelter. We were divided into four groups and came here to Brussels.
>
> We were welcomed by the local Committee, which is temporarily housing us in hotels. Now we have to find us a room and look after ourselves. This is all horrible for us because we are not used to this.
>
> On the one hand, we thank God that we are here and are not brought to some camp. On the other hand, we look ahead with worries. Our waiting number for America is very high and by now we are getting too old to start something new. We are not allowed to work here and it is a pity that daddy cannot use his skills. What are the chances that you can get us an immigration certificate?[9]

With these words of desperation ended the wartime path of communication between Richard and Betty Blum with their sons Seev and Hanan in Palestine. They were not to hear from their parents for another six years. The full details of their story were not made known until January 1945 when Betty Blum, not knowing where in Palestine her sons were now located (due to the precarious security situation in Palestine), wrote a letter from Nice,

France, to relatives (presumably the Brauns, referenced previously by Seev) dwelling in the safety of San Francisco. The first sentence of the account, however, makes it clear that even in writing Betty and Richard Blum are not able to tell all: "Behind us there are so many experiences that we will never put in writing and those who never experienced it will never believe that human beings can create such suffering." (Scott was to notice in their letters that among their experiences the Blums did not put in writing was their imprisonment in Gurs.) The letter continues:

> You remember our trip to Cuba, you remember that we were sent to Brussels, our flight two days ahead of the Germans to Paris? Well, we were caught in Paris by the Germans but escaped to Braudex, and from August '42 we were on the search list to be deported to Poland but we went underground under other names. Everybody was deported from babies to eighty-year-old men and women and it was a most terrible picture to see those people herded and shipped to death. . . .
>
> We had changed many times our domiciles and finally we came to Nice where we had a few months of better conditions under Italian regime. But as the Germans took over it was worse than ever. . . .
>
> The day of our Liberation came on the twenty-eighth of August [1944] as the Americans came to our city and we were free human beings. . . .
>
> We would like to forget what had been between '42 and '44, and to start a new life—but where to go? We have nothing left. We lost everything. But why should we give you those unpleasant reports. . . .
>
> We are more than anxious to contact our boys but we don't have any address.[10]

Their relatives in San Francisco were finally able to put them in contact with Seev, then on Kibbutz Dalia. Betty wrote Seev a letter, *his* first indicator that they had survived the war. In the letter Betty begged Seev to do everything to get her and Richard to Palestine—where they finally landed in safety in 1947.

Under the pile of letters that Seev handed Scott was Richard Blum's membership card in the Union Juive de Resistance (Jewish Resistance Union). "Now where does this fit into the story?" asked Scott. Seev shrugged his shoulders and replied, "I told you, my parents never spoke of what happened to them. If it is not mentioned in their letters, we will likely never know. This Jewish resistance document will remain a mystery—and I'm sure not the only one in my parents' story."

One set of parents, two brothers, two sets of details: some complementary, some different, and some contradictory. The appearance of Seev—the second Blum son—on the scene reminded Sarah and Scott that for every passenger there just may be another unknown person waiting to reveal a missing part of the story that could solve a mystery, or add to it.

In the year between Scott's first contact with Hanan Blum and the eventual encounter with his brother Seev, Sarah and Scott had crossed off still more names from their unaccounted-for list, which now, with the Blums removed, numbered fewer than ten.

17

Displaced Persons

A number of *St. Louis* passengers, having survived the Holocaust, chose to remain in Europe. But many did so while at the same time experiencing and expressing a certain isolation from the environs that became their homes after the war. Very much like Ilse Marcus in Washington Heights, these people remained always displaced persons—emotionally and psychically—despite the fact that they lived long lives in adopted countries over the course of decades. Such was the case with regard to Hannelore Klein, who as a twelve-year-old girl sailed on the *St. Louis* together with her parents Leopold and Luise Klein, her grandparents Karl and Malchen Tannenbaum, and her aunt and cousin, Rosi and Ruth Friedman. Hannelore and all her relatives ended up in the Netherlands after the ship's return to Europe. In 1944 they were deported from Westerbork to Theresienstadt.

At first, Hannelore proved hard to find and her fate hard to discern, despite the fact that the fates of Hannelore's relatives on the *St. Louis* were clear within the pages of available documentary evidence. The record showed that Hannelore's cousin, aunt, and grandparents survived in Theresienstadt. On the central card index of Jews sent to Theresienstadt (prepared by the Beit Theresienstadt memorial in Israel), these family members were listed by the markings "Death: N" and "Survived: Y." Likewise the documentation on Hannelore's parents—who wound up being deported in separate convoys from Theresienstadt to Auschwitz, where they died—was explicit. Sarah and Scott found both Leopold and Luise Klein listed in the Dutch memorial book. These same names turned up in the German *Gedenkbuch* and Berlin *Gedenkbuch*, wherein they were marked as *für tot erklärt* (declared dead).

With regard to Hannelore, however, the researchers were initially stumped by conflicting evidence. "We found her name," Scott recalls, "with matching place and date of birth [Berlin. June 8, 1927] on a postwar alphabetical list of 2,700 Jewish survivors in the Netherlands prepared by the Netherlands Central Registration Office." But contradictory evidence was found in the Beit Theresienstadt central card index of Jews sent to Theresienstadt. The card index listed Hannelore as deported to Auschwitz with the following markings: "Death: Y" and "Survived: N." Still, Sarah and Scott were unable to find Hannelore's name in any of the memorial books where camp victims are listed; nor were they able to find her name on any Auschwitz documentation. "Simply put, we were puzzled by the ambiguity of this case."

Both Sarah and Scott remained perplexed by the discrepancy until one day when Scott received a letter postmarked Amsterdam from a Hannelore Grünberg-Klein. The note began with the words "I am a survivor of the *St. Louis*." In her letter, Hannelore told Scott that a friend in New York had recently sent her a *Washington Post* article about Sarah and Scott's ongoing *St. Louis* research and that Hannelore wanted to make herself known.[1]

Subsequently, during the spring of 2001, Scott made plans to visit Hannelore in her Amsterdam home. "Arranging this interview proved to be complicated. At the time, there was only a small window of opportunity for me to travel to Amsterdam, and Hannelore was scheduled to be at her grandson's bar mitzvah in Israel, in the West Bank settlement of Dolfon, where her daughter Manyu lived." Speaking to Scott on the phone as they arranged their appointment, Hannelore mentioned that her upcoming sojourn promised to be daunting. The Dolfon settlement had been the scene of a number of drive-by shootings by Palestinian militants over the previous months. "I asked her if she was scared," Scott remembers. Hannelore simply replied, "I survived Auschwitz; I'll survive a couple of Palestinian bullets being shot in the air. Now, tell me what days you are available to come over."[2]

Thus an appointment was made, and in due course Scott found himself knocking on the door of Hannelore's spacious row house in a comfortable section of Amsterdam. A smiling

Hannelore, looking much younger than her seventy-three years and with a very spry walk, greeted Scott at the door and then ushered him into the dining room. "The first thing I did was show Hannelore the documents we had found indicating her locations in wartime Europe," Scott recalls. Then he also pulled out Hannelore's index card from Beit Terezin—the one indicating that she did not survive. Hannelore stared at it for a few seconds, and then retorted, "Well, clearly I *did* survive, *and* I'm even alive today."

"So, Mrs. Grünberg," said Scott, "now that I know you are alive, please tell me the story of your survival."

She replied, "My story begins not as survival, but as just normal existence."

An only child, Hannelore's best friend was her cousin Ruth, a year her junior. The two girls were almost like sisters. Growing up on the same street in Berlin, they played together all day long and even dressed in the same way. Their winters were marked by skating lessons; in the summers they swam. Their family was religious, orthodox. Friday evenings and all Jewish holidays were celebrated according to Jewish law. Hannelore's mother, a hearty cook, always prepared elaborate meals. On Shabbat and holidays the family attended the nearby synagogue on Passauer Strasse.

When the Nazis came to power in 1933, Hannelore did not experience any immediate change in her daily life—or at least not any change that she, as a little girl, was aware of. She attended only Jewish schools and thereby did not directly encounter hatred or aggression against Jews from other children or teachers. However, five years later—following Kristallnacht—her world was shattered. Even after the two days of violence subsided and her father had safely avoided the rampaging SA men, he continued to fear being arrested. Afraid to sleep at home, her father stayed with female relatives who were on their own. He felt safer there, believing the Nazis would not search for Jewish men in female-only households.

Hannelore now experienced the fear and anxiety of the time. Even many years later, as she described this time period to Scott, her voice changed in tone, projecting a sense of the darkness of Jewish life under Nazi rule. By 1938 Hannelore was no longer the innocent and unaware schoolgirl she had been in 1933; five years later she had become painfully aware that Jews were being ruthlessly persecuted. For example, her favorite pastimes of skating and swimming were by now prohibited to Jews. As well, her parents were forced to give up their big house and move to her aunt Rosi's small home, where Hannelore's and Ruth's grandparents had also come to live, and from which the entire clan departed to voyage on the *St. Louis* in 1939.

When the *St. Louis* returned to Europe, Hannelore and her family disembarked in Antwerp. They had been assigned to the Netherlands, and like a number of *St. Louis* families, they went at first to the Heyplaat quarantine camp near Rotterdam. The Kleins were only at Heyplaat for six weeks, but sixty years later Hannelore still recalled quite bitterly the "excessive disrespect" exhibited by the Dutch military police regiment who managed the camp. "They were simply anti-Semitic," Hannelore explained. "Today even illegal aliens are treated better in Holland than we were back then."

After Heyplaat, Hannelore and her parents, as well as Aunt Rosi and Ruth, were assigned to the Lloyd Hotel for refugees in Amsterdam, where they shared an apartment. At the same time, Dutch authorities allowed Hannelore's grandparents, Karl and Malchen, to go free because they were over sixty-five years of age. The grandparents moved to a nice apartment, while the Jewish Community of Amsterdam paid for the Kleins' and Friedmans' rooms in the Lloyd Hotel. (In this regard, Hannelore made sure to point out when speaking to Scott that "the Dutch Jews did not want us, which is why they paid for us to be in a hotel — far away from them." As Scott was quick to notice, even amidst the freedom she enjoyed all the years in the Netherlands since the war, Hannelore was still not fully acculturated into the Dutch Jewish milieu. "Until this day, I feel like a *German* Jew," Hannelore told him, "not a Dutch Jew.")

Boredom colored Hannelore and Ruth's days at the Lloyd Hotel; there was little to do for fun. As well, Hannelore's parents were depressed, especially her father. Being unemployed, he saw no future. The family existed on very little money. "Today everybody gets handouts, but at that time the Dutch did not like refugees. There were a lot of narrow-minded people who did not want to help us." Hannelore's one pleasant memory from these days was of attending school. Children from the Lloyd Hotel went to a Jewish school in the southern part of Amsterdam. Hannelore and Ruth studied in a special track focused on learning the Dutch language. (Hannelore told Scott she remembered telling the other students about the *St. Louis,* "but everybody there had their own story.")

Ten uneventful months went by with the Klein family living at the Lloyd Hotel. Then everything changed—at once and forever—in May 1940 when the Germans swept into the Netherlands. "I said to mother 'Can we hide from the Nazis?' My mother answered, 'No. We must always stick together.' But, until this day, I believe that it would have been possible to hide." Within days of the German occupation, Hannelore and her parents were transferred by ship and by truck to the Westerbork internment camp, a twelve-hour journey. Hannelore commented to Scott, "My mother, *always afraid,* did not like the idea of our going to Westerbork, as it was too near the German border." Her father, who felt he had nothing to lose from the doldrums of life in Amsterdam, was more positive. The balance of Hannelore's family—her grandparents, her aunt, and her cousin—would eventually follow the Kleins to Westerbork in July 1942.

Shortly after Hannelore's family arrived at the camp, Leopold became a barrack leader, responsible for organizing furniture, supplies, and food. The Kleins lived in a tiny family barracks and carried their meals to the barracks from a central kitchen. Once a week they were assigned a time for a shower. Early in their incarceration at Westerbork, the family was allowed permits for Sunday hikes in the woods. At the same time—like other *St. Louis* children—Hannelore became involved in the camp's Zionist youth organization. There were, Hannelore told Scott, "no real sorrows. Nasty things passed us by."

Beginning in mid-1942, however, "nasty things" stopped passing by the inmates at Westerbork, including Hannelore and her *chaverim* (comrades) in the youth movement. As has been previously recounted, German authorities assumed direct control of Westerbork during the summer. Sunday trips to the woods ceased. Beginning at age fourteen, all camp inmates had to work sixty hours a week in the fields. Additionally, whole families were now crowded into a single room. The Germans also launched devastating deportations to Auschwitz and Sobibór. The convoys departed every Tuesday, creating an atmosphere of

Hannelore Klein with her parents, Luise and Leopold, in the Westerbork transit camp during World War II. (USHMM, courtesy of Hannelore Grünberg-Klein)

constant tension and anxiety. "Barrack leaders on Mondays called out names for transports," Hannelore recalled. But the names of Hannelore and her family members never turned up on the convoy lists for the two killing centers. They remained at Westerbork for another year and a half, until the beginning of 1944, when word came that there would soon be a very large transport to the Theresienstadt ghetto—this to include special categories of Jews. Soon Hannelore and all her extended family received instructions to go on this "priority" transport, evidently because her father had won the Iron Cross fighting for Germany during World War I.

Arriving in Theresienstadt—the same "showplace" ghetto where the Finks and other *St. Louis* families also spent time— Hannelore and her kin were assigned to a dormitory in the attic of a barracks. Soon thereafter the entire family—save for the grandparents—was registered for work. Hannelore and Ruth took care of toddlers from the Netherlands. Leopold and Karl picked up papers from the streets with long pointed sticks. And Luise and Rosi served as caretakers in the ghetto's orphanage. During her talk with Scott, Hannelore recalled that a Zionist youth leader from Westerbork, Leo Blumson, came to

Theresienstadt in the same transport with Hannelore and her family. "So we were able to have a few Jewish meetings—where we talked about Jewish literature and sang Jewish songs—but these were much more difficult to orchestrate than they had been in Westerbork. As for me, all I thought of was living in Palestine after the war. I had no thought of not surviving."

Survival became more of a question, however, on September 28, 1944—the day after Yom Kippur—when the Germans prepared a transport for Auschwitz that was to carry virtually all of the Jewish men in the camp, save for the elderly. While Hannelore's grandfather received an exemption, Hannelore's father was made to board the train. "My mother thought I could get my father off the train. She was desperate, delusional," Hannelore remembered. Luise instructed Hannelore—seventeen, blonde, and pretty—to plead with the ghetto commandant to let her father stay in Theresienstadt. Though Hannelore desperately wanted to save her father, she nevertheless held back. "I froze in place." To approach the commandant she would have had to enter the area where the SS guards patrolled the trains. Such action was strictly forbidden on the threat of death and would, Hannelore realized, have been pointless. If she tried to approach the commandant, she would not only fail but would also quite likely pay with her life for trying. "My mother and I were deported the next week on a crowded train. I could hardly stand. I had to squat." All Hannelore and Luise carried between them was one backpack and a meager amount of food. Luise Klein had been in shock since her husband had been deported the week before. She appeared not to know what was going on around her. During the three-day trip to Auschwitz she just stared vacantly into space.

It was night when they arrived in Auschwitz-Birkenau. Describing the scene for Scott, Hannelore recalled that there was no bush, tree, or green thing to be seen. The place seemed desolate and silent as she and her mother joined the long line of women and children queued up before several SS commanders. When Hannelore and Luise got to the head of the line, one of the officers gestured for Luise to go to the left and for Hannelore to go to the right. "My mother and I were separated ten to twenty meters from the train. My mother was in a daze. Like a ghost. My mother could see but could not see *me*. She looked right through me. I turned to one of the officers and said, 'I want to be with my mother.' He answered: 'You'll see her this evening.'" Luise, meanwhile, followed along with the long line of women marching slowly to the left. Hannelore waited and watched as long as she could, but her mother did not look back.

After undressing, showering, and being shaved by other prisoners, Hannelore donned her camp uniform and entered the barracks to which she'd been assigned. There another woman from the transport embraced her in tears, explaining what Hannelore had not yet guessed: that Luise and all who walked with her—among them the woman's own mother and two young daughters—had been dispatched to the Auschwitz gas chambers. The two women held onto to each other and wept. (A little while later, Hannelore briefly encountered some of the Gruenthals from the *St. Louis*. "They were all so disoriented. I slept in the same barracks with Ruthild, but she did not even recognize me.") Throughout all this, however, Hannelore made a point of maintaining her focus. "I still never doubted my survival, not for one minute."

Hannelore was only at Auschwitz a few weeks before the SS shipped her out to Germany along with other young women, all of them to serve as slave laborers in an airplane factory near Dresden. "I saw Dresden burning," she recalls of February 1945, "but I had no clue that liberation was imminent." Whenever air-raid sirens sounded, guards locked the women workers from Auschwitz on the top floor of the factory—a likely target of Allied bombers—while the SS took refuge in a shelter. Then, in the early spring of 1945, the women found themselves being moved again by cattle car. During this journey, rations consisted of a spoon of sugar a day and just a little water. Whenever the train stopped— usually just once each day—the women rushed to drink water from streams and to relieve themselves. They grew weaker and sicker as the train kept going, finally arriving at the Mauthausen concentration camp in the mountains of upper Austria. Here they remained for several weeks—barely existing on the sparsest of rations—until the Americans finally liberated the site.

When the end came and the women were free, they did not cheer or express joy. ("What were you thinking when the liberation came?" Scott asked Hannelore. "Not much," she answered. "Only about food.") Gathering her strength under the care of

American soldiers, Hannelore spent some time visiting a friend and former bunkmate from the airplane factory, Reni Guttman, who had fallen ill with typhoid. As a gift, Reni gave Hannelore her only possession: a soapbox with her initials fashioned out of airplane metal. When Hannelore found a discarded raincoat cast on the ground outside the camp, she fashioned herself a carrying bag. She put Reni's gift and the few other possessions, including her bread rations, into this bag. Not long thereafter she left Mauthausen. Hannelore never saw or heard from Reni again.

Learning from the International Red Cross that her grandparents, aunt, and cousin had all survived the war, Hannelore eventually—after a lengthy stay of several months at a refugee camp in France—returned to Amsterdam in October 1945. The Central Station in Amsterdam was nearly empty when Hannelore got off the train, but a representative of a Jewish agency waited to receive her. He gave her twenty-five Dutch guilders, crossed her name off a list, and took her to a car that brought her to her family. In the days that followed, Hannelore shared a big bed with her grandparents but did not share thoughts or regrets concerning the loss of her parents. On this subject there was only silence. Although Hannelore had long dreamed of immigrating to Palestine, she ultimately decided to stay in the Netherlands in order to be near what remained of her family. A few years later she married another German Jew.

Looking back on her experiences, Hannelore told Scott she bore no grudge against the United States. "In terms of America, I only have resentment against FDR." She heaped praise on the American Jewish community, who did so much—through the JDC—to help the *St. Louis* passengers during and after the voyage. She reserved her greatest resentment for the very place where she had lived the balance of her life: the Netherlands. Decades after the fact, it still rankled Hannelore that Dutch Jews, in her estimation, did little to support and protect émigré Jews in the time of crisis. She likewise could not forget the many Dutch non-Jews who aided and abetted the Nazis. "I feel my real home is Israel, though after all these years I feel more *at home* in Holland." Commenting that she did not know "where God was" during the Holocaust, Hannelore told Scott that now "the miracle of Israel" served as the focus of her faith. Israel, she told Scott, symbolized all that was hopeful for Jews in the post-Holocaust world. "My daughter may be living around barbed-wire [to protect her community from attack], but she is better off than she would be here in Holland. There is no Jewish future here."

Another *St. Louis* survivor, Julius Fanto, also lived out his days in Europe after the war. His story came to Sarah and Scott via publicity in the *New York Times.*

As had been the case with Hannelore, finding Julius proved to be a challenge. Indeed, Mr. Fanto seemed a riddle from the very start. First of all, his name always stood out on the passenger manifest because it sounded Italian. Despite this, surviving documents indicated he was born in Wradist, Poland, on June 26, 1892. To complicate matters further, Fanto's name appeared under the Czech quota in *St. Louis* documents related to applications for U.S. visas. Beyond these bits of information, Scott and Sarah knew very little about Fanto, who traveled alone on the ship and was among the passengers eventually sent to Belgium. After the voyage, there was evidence that Fanto either was deported (as an enemy alien) or migrated from Belgium to France.

Checks at the National Archives revealed no record of Julius Fanto immigrating to the United States after World War II. Nevertheless—armed with the information that a Ludwig Fanto living at 36 Newark Street, Hoboken, had signed Julius's U.S. visa application in 1939—Scott spent some time looking through the phone books of northern New Jersey searching for various Fanto connections. There was no Ludwig Fanto listed for Hoboken or, indeed, anywhere else in the United States. Scott did, however, run across several Fantos in the phone book for Jersey City, not far from Hoboken. When Scott dialed the first of these listings, he wound up talking to a woman who knew nothing of the *St. Louis,* had no relative named Ludwig, and told Scott not to bother calling any of the other Fantos in Jersey, because they were all related and were all Italian. "The men in my family are Anthonys, Luigis, and Marios; there are no Ludwigs."[3] Ringing off, Scott at this point figured he would never find Julius Fanto or anyone connected with him.

The next day, however, an article about Sarah, Scott, and their quest appeared in the *New York Times.* At the researchers' request, the item included a listing of unaccounted-for passengers. Within hours of the piece hitting the streets, Scott received a message on

his answering machine from an Elizabeth Bergstein in Manhattan, who identified herself as Julius Fanto's niece. In a subsequent discussion, Scott learned that Ms. Bergstein was aware of
the Fantos in New Jersey, "but we are not related; they are Italian." She did not know how her family got the name Fanto, as
they were Jews from Poland who eventually settled in Austria.[4]
Neither did she know why her Uncle Julius had been listed
under the Czech quota. "This must just have been a mistake,"
she said. "The Fanto family has no Czech connections at all." Ms.
Bergstein told Scott that she had been born in Vienna in 1938.
Shortly thereafter her parents fled to England and then to the
United States. She still clung to distant and vague memories of
her uncle, Ludwig Fanto, older brother to both Julius and to
Bergstein's mother. She likewise recalled his home in Hoboken,
even though she was only two years old when he died in 1940.

Ms. Bergstein thought it ironic that her Uncle Julius had been
forced to leave Austria, the adopted country he so loved. "He
was very patriotic." Julius had fought for the Austro-Hungarian
Empire in World War I, serving near the Mirano area of northern
Italy. After the war he settled in Vienna and worked for the Aus-
trian National Railroad. She believed he left Vienna in 1938—
about the same time as her parents—seeking exit to North America via Germany. Bergstein did not know the circumstances, or
the exact timing, of her uncle's coming to France from Belgium in
the early 1940s, but she remembered that he eventually hid out in
the home of non-Jewish friends near Marseille.

At the time Julius booked passage on the *St. Louis,* he had a
longtime girlfriend named Hilde, who was not Jewish. In fact,
she came from a Nazi family who heartily disapproved of her
beau. After the war, Julius returned to Vienna, started a business,
and continued to see his Hilde, whose family never accepted
him. The couple eventually married, finally formalizing a long-
standing relationship in 1960 or 1961, when they were both approaching age seventy.

Ms. Bergstein visited Julius several times in Vienna, and Julius made one extended six-week visit to the United States in
1959. She recalled her uncle as a very astute and gracious gentleman who spoke English fluently. She also recalled the home
where Julius and Hilde lived in their later years. Julius and
Hilde's rooms took up the third floor of Hilde's old family villa, a

Julius Fanto (standing on left) during his service in World War I. (USHMM, courtesy of Elizabeth Bergstein)

structure then owned by one of Hilde's nephews, himself an un-repentant Nazi who refused to speak with Julius and likewise made a point of ignoring Julius's visiting relatives from the States. Julius died in 1974, and his wife soon thereafter. They are buried in the Central Cemetery, one of Vienna's three primary Jewish cemeteries.

"I hope the story of my uncle helps the tale of the *St. Louis* to endure," Ms. Bergstein said in a phone interview. "It was a ter-rible thing what Roosevelt did, sending those people back to Hit-ler. It was a great crime, a tragedy. Think of the lives lost."[5]

A German Jew living in the Netherlands over long decades, feeling alienated from Germany, but also feeling alienated from the Dutch Jews by whom she has been surrounded most of her life. A Polish Jew who, as a young man, adopted a fierce national-ist instinct for his adopted country of Austria, then survived the Holocaust only to confront outright Nazi anti-Semitism yet again beneath the very same roof under which he slept each night. In a way, both were equally adrift in their life after the Holocaust, lacking any place to call their true homeland.

18

Kew Gardens Portrait

A Song at Auschwitz

It is a crisp spring day, and Scott's destination is a nicely maintained, red-brick building just around the corner from the impressive Queens County Courthouse in Kew Gardens, New York. Arriving at the door of an apartment on the second floor, the researcher is invited in by a smiling and youthful woman in her sixties, Judith Steel.

Born Judith Koeppel in Berlin in 1938, Ms. Steel spent her adolescence and adulthood in the United States. During the folk boom of the 1960s, she began writing and singing songs, accompanying herself on guitar. Today she is a cantor at her local synagogue and also a third-degree professional Master of Reiki. (Pronounced *ray-key*—Japanese for "universal energy"—Reiki is an ancient healing modality that, according to Judith, "balances, purifies and ultimately heals the body, mind, and spirit through the gentle transference of energy, positive energy, from practitioner to client.")

A massage table, used for Reiki, takes up a full third of what at times doubles as Judith's dining room. On an opposite wall hangs a collection of old publicity photos and posters from Judith's career as a folksinger. Near these on the same wall hangs a collection of family snapshots. "I've got pictures here of all three of my families," she says. One aging print shows her parents, Josef and Irmgard Koeppel, carrying her at age fourteen months aboard the *St. Louis*. Another displays the profile of her grandfather, Jacob Koeppel, who accompanied them on the same

Irmgard, Josef, Jacob, and Judith Koeppel on board the *St. Louis*, May 1939. (USHMM, courtesy of Judith Koeppel Steel)

voyage. Beside this we see a picture of Judith age seven with her "French family"—"righteous Gentiles" who sheltered her and protected her after her birth parents were taken away. And next to that, in a matching frame, we have the teenage Judith sitting with a tanned, middle aged German American couple, her birth father's brother and the brother's wife whom she introduces as "my mom and dad."

One last photo, positioned just above the shot of baby Judith on the *St. Louis* with Josef and Irmgard, shows the adult Judith strumming her guitar and singing a song at an unlikely place: the gates of Auschwitz. "Most people have graveyards where they can go and be near their parents," she says. "I have Auschwitz. I wrote my mother and father a song and sang it for them there, thanking them for saving me. It was more than just a song, really. It was a prayer, my way of saying Kaddish for them. You see, that's as close as I can come to those dear people, there at that terrible place, Auschwitz."[1]

Sitting down at one end of a long couch in her living room, Judith quickly announces that she recollects nothing about the voyage of the *St. Louis*. "I was just a baby," she explains. "All that I remember—and even that is vague—came after. I am told that following the return of the ship my parents and I were assigned to France. My earliest memories are all French. When I was three and four we were living in a small town in the Pyrenees. I remember my mother as very loving, smiling, playful, and soft-spoken. I remember my father as more serious—not a disciplinarian, but more somber than my mother. I recall dark features and a receding hairline. He looks much older, in my memories, than he does in his picture taken aboard ship. My grandfather was also always with us, and he—in my memory—is complete gentleness and love."

During their time in the Pyrenees, the Koeppels became close friends with the family in whose house they rented a small apartment, a Catholic couple with a daughter, Suzi, four years older than Judith. "The parents were named Eletta and Joseph Enard. And Eletta—whom I always called 'Mama Suzi' for some reason, probably because it was my very little girl's way of saying 'Suzi's mother'—was very nice to me. I would call out to her from our window when I would see her hanging out her laundry. 'Mama Suzi, would you like me to come over?' You see, I was very relaxed and happy. I didn't know we were in hiding. I didn't realize we were on the run from anything. I just played. I had fun. There were lots of other children around and everyone was nice. But now, thinking back, I realize why my father always seemed so serious and so anxious."

Judith's carefree world changed forever before dawn one morning at the beginning of September 1942 when the Vichy police pounded on the door, entered the apartment, and took Judith and her parents into custody. "I was woken up," she recalls, "and there was a lot of confusion. My grandfather was in bed. The police weren't taking him; he was too frail to be moved. My mother let me go over to him to say goodbye. When I said goodbye, he was crying. He couldn't even speak. I remember telling him: 'Please don't cry, Opa. I'll be back soon.' I didn't understand what was happening. I just knew I was going somewhere with my parents. As long as I had my parents, I was not terrified."

This same innocence shielded Judith when the Germans—to whom the Vichy police immediately handed over the Koeppels—sent them to the camp at Gurs. Formerly a French-operated refugee camp, Gurs was now a Vichy-run first stop on the terrible road that led eventually to Drancy and then Auschwitz. During the brief time they were with their daughter at Gurs, Judith's parents made light of the many stern, armed men who patrolled the place. "They are here to keep us safe," they told their daughter. The same, it seemed, went for the barbed wire that surrounded them. "My parents tried to protect me from the fact that we were in bondage," says Judith. "I never sensed any fear in them whatsoever until just before I never saw them again."

Judith's memories of her last hours with her parents—unlike most other memories from her early childhood—are crystal clear. They had been at Gurs for less than a week. She recalls playing with her mother on a cot in one of the large, squalid bunkers in which the hundreds of internees lived.

> My mother was bouncing me on her knee, and we were having a wonderful time. And then, all of a sudden, she stopped bouncing me, and to this day I cannot forget the look in her eyes. She looked at me and she said, in German, something like: "Judy, you may never see Mommy and Daddy again." And she said she just wished for me to grow up and be happy and have a good life. I didn't, of course, want to believe it. I just threw my arms

around her and said: "Mommy, Mommy, don't be silly. Nothing's going to happen. We're together. Let's play. Let's play." Then she continued to play with me, but I can't forget the look in her eyes. There was so much sadness, so much sadness. And it must have taken a lot of courage for her to continue playing with me at that time.

A little bit later, after night had fallen, Judith's father came, took her by the hand, and said lightheartedly: "Come on, Judy. Let's take a little walk." In the same moment, Judith's smiling mother quickly pecked her on the cheek and, in a tone meant to reassure, said: "Bye, bye. Have a good time." It seemed to Judith that she and her father walked a considerable distance in the darkness before they came to a place "where there was some light and some people." Judith found out years later that the men whom her father greeted were members of the Oeuvre de Secours aux Enfants (OSE). "They were trying to get as many children out of the camp as possible, because they'd received word that new transports were going to start leaving Gurs for Drancy, and then Auschwitz, very shortly. I've been told recently that they had to bribe the guards at the camp to let them take the children out, so much per head."

Judith stood there in the night with her father for what seemed a long time, watching people come and go. "He was holding my hand, my left hand," she recalls. "Somebody gave me something hot to drink, I think hot chocolate. I was holding that in my right hand, and at some point my attention was diverted to my right side. My father said, 'Look over there, look over there,' and there must have been something distracting me. I kept looking and then I heard my father say, 'just a minute, Judy,' and he dropped my hand. Then my hand was picked up again, and I assumed it was my father, but when I turned around it was someone else holding my hand. I never saw my father again after that. I screamed 'Where's my Daddy? Where's my Daddy?' And the answer was, 'Don't worry, he'll be back.' But that's when my panic started."

Up to that moment, Judith had no inkling of what was about to happen. "My mother had tried to warn me, I guess, in a very sweet way. But a child doesn't understand these things." Soon, she found herself in a small room with other children also just separated from their incarcerated parents. They all screamed and

Judith Koeppel with her grandfather Jacob while in hiding in Nay, France, c. 1942. (USHMM, courtesy of Judith Koeppel Steel)

cried along with Judith, until, in time, they lay down exhausted and fell asleep. "I think the drink they had given us, the hot chocolate I was sipping when my father dropped my hand, might have had something in it."

During the night, while they slept, the OSE workers moved the children to a secret location outside the bounds of the Gurs camp; thankfully the next day Judith opened her eyes to someone she knew well, Joseph Enard. "He was a comforting sight. I was *very* glad to see him. He drove me back to the Pyrenees, and I saw my grandfather who was still with the Enards. He held me in his arms and cried, overjoyed. Then I gave a big hug to Mama Suzi. She had been very good to me before I lost my parents, and this was to continue. My mother, I learned later, had asked her to take care of me should anything happen, and Mama Suzi fulfilled that promise."[2]

For a time, Judith would sporadically ask when her mother and father would be returning, but the Enards' answers were always vague and noncommittal. "After a while I just stopped asking." Judith and the Enards' daughter shared a bedroom. In a few months, Eletta gave birth to a son. "I was treated as one of them. The Enards always did their best for me."

Judith remained with Eletta and her family until the end of the war. Her grandfather died of natural causes in late 1943. Largely to protect Judith from detection, Joseph and Eletta took her to Roman Catholic mass regularly, but they never allowed her to forget her true identity as a Jew. Once the war was over, the Enards—who seemed to simply *know* that Judith's parents were dead, though they never explicitly said so—arranged for the nearly eight-year-old girl to go to Josef Koeppel's brother in the United States, where he lived in Washington Heights in New York City. "I've been an American ever since. A typical American kid. And I've had a good life, as my mother wished that I would."

Judith stayed in touch with the Enards. She entertained the elderly Eletta in New York in the 1980s, and she also arranged for the names of both Joseph and Eletta to be inscribed on the Wall of Honor in the Garden of the Righteous at Yad Vashem in Jerusalem. "If they had ever been discovered hiding me," says Judith, "they could have been killed, and their daughters as well. I am here because of the bravery of the Enards, and because of my parents' bravery. Think how hard it must have been for

Judith Koeppel (center with hat) with other Jewish children rescued by the OSE preparing to board a ship for the United States, Marseille, France, 1946. (OSE Archive, courtesy of Centre de Documentation Juive Contemporaine)

my parents to give me up *and* for the Enards to risk everything by sheltering me; but they all, the four of them, made those sacrifices and took those risks so that I could live."

19

The Missing

After seven years of research, in late 2003, there remained just one passenger of the *St. Louis* whose fate Sarah and Scott had yet to unearth. This was Rosalie Moser—born Rosalie Moses on April 15, 1877, in Horn, Czechoslovakia—who sailed on the *St. Louis* with her husband, Edmund Moser, born June 20, 1871, in Helmstedt, Germany. The couple had lived in Prague for quite some time before their departure on the *St. Louis.* Upon the ship's return to Europe, the Mosers were sent to France, but no other details of their wartime experience were immediately available.

Postwar documents reveal that Edmund Moser survived the Holocaust and eventually came to the United States. Immigration files at the National Archives indicate that he flew alone from Paris and arrived in New York City on September 17, 1947. Edmund's immigration documents list him as stateless and retired, with a previous address on rue Victor Hugo in Perigueux, France. According to the U.S. Immigration and Naturalization Service, "There is no evidence of naturalization and no other information is available."[1]

Edmund Moser's encounter with America was fleeting. He died a little over a year after arriving in the United States. Health Department Records show him as passing away in Manhattan on November 16, 1948.

With regard to Rosalie, Sarah and Scott's first thought was that she might have come to the United States on a flight other than Edmund's, or on a ship. However, diligent checks of immigration records revealed only a Rosa Moser, someone whose age did not match that of the *St. Louis* passenger. Sarah and Scott also turned up seven "hits"—using both Rosalie's married and maiden names—in the Social Security Death Benefits Index (SSDI), but none was the woman from the *St. Louis*. Then Scott checked records at Manhattan's Vital Statistics Bureau to see if Edmund Moser left a will. Scott found no will, suggesting that Rosalie stayed or died in Europe. The absence of a will also suggested that the couple had no children, hence erasing the possibility of yet another solid lead. Meanwhile, surviving *St. Louis* passengers offered tips and advice. Ruth Heilbrun wrote Scott: "Mr. and Mrs. Moser could be the parents of Dr. Moser who lives in Queens, New York, and my friend *St. Louis* passenger Jane Keibel who lives in Kew Gardens sees him on occasion."[2] Herbert Karliner thought Rosalie Moser "might be related to the Moser family in Poughkeepsie."[3] But neither of these leads panned out. Thus Sarah and Scott were left with a nagging question: If *St. Louis* passengers did not know what happened to Rosalie, who would?

The answer to that question perhaps was not to be found in the United States but back in France, where the Mosers spent the war years under conditions that were still a mystery to Sarah and Scott. Why not, thought Sarah and Scott, work backward in terms of the little they knew about the couple's whereabouts in France? As previously stated, their last known address was in Périgueux, in the rural Dordogne region of southwestern France, near the vineyards of Bordeaux. Via a researcher in France, Sarah and Scott immediately had a letter of inquiry sent to the local archives in Périgueux (Archive communales de Périgueux). Within a very short time, they received some very revealing pieces of information from the archive.

One was a document from the Hôpital des Réfugiés de la Dordogne, in Clairvivre (part of Périgueux, in the commune of Salagnac) dated May 5, 1942, stating that "Rosalie Moser is very sick." (As a side note, this document, interestingly and contrary to prior assumptions, mentioned that Edmond Moser has a daughter who lives in the United States who was providing a subsidy for her parents. On a previous line in the same document, it says that Rosalie has no children. Perhaps this was a daughter from a previous marriage?)

The second and corroborating document was dated a little earlier, March 1, 1942, from a Doctor J.-L. LaVille at the same hospital, stating that Rosalie had been admitted to the emergency room to have a surgery of the intestines and that a second surgery had already been scheduled.[4]

Sarah and Scott were left hanging. It was not clear from Dr. La Ville's description precisely *when* the initial surgery had taken place and *if* the second surgery ever occurred. Nevertheless, this documentation was indeed quite suggestive. Sarah and Scott could perhaps make the assumption, based on her relatively advanced age in 1942 and the fact that her husband came to the United States without her, that Rosalie Moser died in the hospital. But absent a piece of paper, they certainly could not say for sure.

Sarah and Scott then contacted the Archives Départementales de Dordogne in search of any document mentioning Edmund or Rosalie Moser. This archive was to provide Sarah and Scott with an additional lead as to Rosalie's fate. The document that the Dordogne archive sent to Washington stated that Edmund Moser was a widower when he left France. No trace could be found of Rosalie in this archive, but certainly this statement on Edmund would imply that Rosalie had died.[5]

Still, this was only negative information, so Sarah and Scott could still not be sure. They needed to find some sort of hospital record. They were not optimistic on this count, since who knows for how long hospitals keep records? And, in wartime and under military occupation, perhaps there were none. They needed to find someone local—a resident of Périgueux—who could do leg work for them and check hospital records, *if* wartime hospital records actually existed. As luck would have it, the Oral History Department of the Holocaust Museum had a person who conducted survivor interviews in Périgueux. Perhaps she could assist Sarah and Scott. Emerging from initial contact with the interviewer was the piece of news that she had moved away from Périgueux six months earlier and now lived near Toulouse. She would however, be back visiting Périgueux the following Monday and would gladly check to see what hospital records, if any, existed.

The records, in fact, existed and were found in the Périgueux Registry Office of the very same refugee hospital. Sarah and Scott shortly thereafter received in the mail the following document, dated June 3, 1942:

The third of June nineteen hundred forty two at 9 A.M. Rosalie Moser née Moses, born in Detmoldt (Germany) the fifteenth of April eighteen hundred seventy seven, no profession, daughter of Hermann Moses and Bertha Rosenbaum, wife of Edmond Moser, domiciled 87 rue Chancy, Périgueux, refugee from Le Mans (Sarthe), 15 rue de la Sciérie, died at the refugees' hospital of the Dordogne in Clairvivre, in the commune of Salagnac.

Drawn up June fourth nineteen hundred forty two at 10 A.M. on the declaration of Mr. Henri Fillhard, aged fifty nine, head of the registry office of the refugees' hospital of the Dordogne, who read it and signed it with me, François Caille, Mayor of Salagnac.[6]

On one level, this piece of information ended for Sarah and Scott what had become an eight-year quest to determine the fates of all 937 *St. Louis* passengers. Rosalie Moser, the last missing passenger, was now accounted for. Simply, and sadly, she died in a French hospital in 1942. But did the search really end there? Shouldn't Sarah and Scott pursue people, eyewitnesses, who actually knew Rosalie Moser in the hopes that they could fill in gaps and add a more detailed degree of certainty to her story? Or by doing this would they open themselves up to contradictions in the story?

There was a precedent for this concern. Take the case of Fritz Zweigenthal. It seemed, at times, the more Sarah and Scott found out about passenger Fritz Zweigenthal, the less they actually knew about him. If there had been one unaccounted-for passenger who could qualify for the top of the "most wanted missing passenger" list, it would have been Zweigenthal. The last name on the alphabetical list of 937 *St. Louis* passengers, his case aroused Sarah and Scott's attention from day one. Little was known about this man. He was born on June 8, 1909, in Vienna, where he lived through 1939. Zweigenthal disembarked in Belgium after the *St. Louis* returned to Europe. On a JDC list of *St. Louis* passengers in Belgium dated May 1940, his visa status is marked as category "C": "to receive visa within next three months." Around that time, however, Fritz was sent by Belgian authorities to the St. Cyprien internment camp in France. In October 1940, he was transferred from St. Cyprien to the Gurs internment camp. Sarah and Scott presumed that as of January 1941 he was still in Gurs because they found his name on a Gurs prisoner list dated January 24, 1941. Past this date, the name Fritz Zweigenthal never resurfaced on a wartime document.

After four years of searching, Sarah and Scott had stumbled on no clues, no leads. Fritz's family name turned out to be extremely unusual. They could find only three people in the world with the name Zweigenthal: one in New York, who said that Zweigenthal was a made-up name the family took at Ellis Island; one in Los Angeles, who knew of no *Fritz* Zweigenthal and who had changed the family name to Zentall; and one in Haifa, Israel, who had never heard of passenger Fritz Zweigenthal.

Then, reaping the blessings of technology at the turn of the twenty-first century, Sarah came across a newly computerized list of testimonies at Yad Vashem. In 1954, Yad Vashem began collecting forms from survivors and others who wished to record information about family and friends who had perished in the Holocaust. The institution then began computerizing those forms on a small scale in September 1991. By 1999, it had completed the computerization of more than one million pages, which are now accessible to the public in the new Yad Vashem archives reading room. After spending countless hours during a number of visits to Israel at the Yad Vashem archives, combing time and again through Red Cross and other postwar lists of names, Sarah was finally able to access personal information on victims provided by those who knew them.

On March 8, 2000, Sarah discovered that these newly accessible "Pages of Testimony" were a treasure trove of information for the search project, beginning with Fritz Zweigenthal. In 1955, a resident of Tel Aviv named Isadore Klaber provided testimony to Yad Vashem on Fritz Zweigenthal. Isadore Klaber was Fritz's uncle. He reported that his nephew died in a concentration camp in France. Sixteen years later, in 1971, a resident of the Bronx named Ernst Zweigenthal also provided testimony to Yad Vashem. Ernst, who was Fritz Zweigenthal's brother, reported that Fritz died in 1942 in Auschwitz. Their contrary accounts were somewhat understandable since the majority of Jews deported from France were sent to Auschwitz and Ernst may have simply inferred that is what happened.

After hearing Sarah's report, Scott's only thought was to find these people—first, brother Ernst. Being that Scott and Sarah had already located and spoken to all the Zweigenthals in the world listed in telephone directories, they proceeded straight to the SSDI. They discovered that Ernst Zweigenthal died on August 18, 1972, exactly ten months after he passed on his testimony to Yad Vashem. And, as listed in SSDI, Ernst's wife died in 1987.

After an unsuccessful attempt to find their next of kin by accessing their will at the Bronx County Surrogate's Court ("Nothing on file," the records clerk told Sarah and Scott. "It must have been lost. It happens sometimes."), and after dismissing the idea of going to Ernst's west Bronx neighborhood to look for clues (a neighborhood, unlike Washington Heights, now depleted of its former Jewish population), Sarah and Scott were assisted by the director of a New York City Jewish funeral home conglomerate, who faxed them the following information: "Ernst Zweigenthal died August 18, 1972. He was buried on August 20 in King Solomon Cemetery, Clifton, NJ. His wife, Sidelle Zweigenthal, was buried next to him on June 18, 1987. Next of kin designated as Sidelle's sister Ruth P., Beekman St. in Manhattan."

Sarah and Scott then called Ruth and asked what she could tell them about Fritz Zweigenthal. "Who?" she asked. "Ernst's brother Fritz," they explained. Her reply: "I never even knew that Ernst had a brother." She said that Ernst and his wife had no children and that she had no further information.

A few minutes later, Sarah and Scott received a telephone call from Ruth's daughter. She was suspicious of their efforts, would not give her name, and requested that they not bother her eighty-three-year-old mother. She also asked Sarah and Scott why they were looking for her uncle after all this time. When they explained the *St. Louis* search project to her, she did say she remembered her Uncle Ernst mentioning a brother who died "in the war" but nothing more. She also added that her mother was mistaken. In fact, Ernst did have a child, though she said she did not know the name and would not reveal the sex. Sarah and Scott did not know whom to believe and came to the realization that they were at the end of the informational line in terms of what could be gleaned from the Zweigenthals on this side of the ocean.

Clearly now was the time to pursue the search for Isadore Klaber, Fritz Zweigenthal's uncle in Tel Aviv who submitted the other piece of testimony to Yad Vashem on Fritz's wartime fate. Following a long road in this pursuit, including a 2001 visit to

Isadore Klaber's former Tel Aviv residence at 12 Zerubavel Street (a street swarming with security guards that day, immediately following a terrorist suicide bombing at a nearby disco); waiting on long lines to obtain real estate deeds at the Tel Aviv Land and Settlement Office; and an unsuccessful attempt at locating a death record at the Tel Aviv Hevra Kadisha (Burial Society) closed for construction, Sarah and Scott were finally able to locate a grandson of Isadore Klaber—not in Tel Aviv but in New York.

The nephew's name was Adam Klaber, and he was as excited that he had been found as were Sarah and Scott. "Fritz Zweigenthal. Of course I know Fritz Zweigenthal. He was my father's first cousin, as of course was Ernst."[7] Adam then related to Sarah and Scott that Ernst and Sidelle, who had sponsored Adam's grandfather Isadore Klaber to Palestine in the 1930s, indeed had no children. Ernst himself was able to immigrate to the United States in the 1930s, leaving behind his brother Fritz and mother, Regina. Fritz then left Vienna to sail on the *St. Louis;* Regina perished in the Holocaust.

Over a cell phone, Adam was able to clear up a number of lingering discrepancies and questions about Ernst. But what about Fritz, the mystery *St. Louis* passenger? *He* was really the person being sought. Sarah and Scott would have to wait a few days. Adam knew Ernst personally; Fritz, however, was a name from the past, so Adam would have to check his family tree at home. Calling back a few days later, Adam shared the following report from his father's entry in the family tree: "Fritz Zweigenthal was born on December 22, 1907, in Vienna. He had a twin brother, Ernst. ["A twin?" Sarah and Scott thought. "Such a basic thing they did not know about this man who had captivated their attention and imagination for so long."] His parents were Regina Klaber and Arnold Zweigenthal. His father died in 1928 in Austria, and Regina died in the Holocaust. No one knows how Fritz died; he was in Vienna and may have escaped to France but disappeared. We believe he was killed in the Holocaust since he never surfaced." In Adam's words: "Related to Fritz, this is all I have from my father."

It is not clear from Adam's father's account if he even knew that Fritz was on the *St. Louis.* In any case, for Adam Klaber's father to know that Fritz was in France during the war, he must have heard something, or received some written information.

That clue seemed to have been swept up by sixty intervening years.

Adam had one possible lead left to offer. Fritz had a first cousin, an Edith (Klaber) DeZeeuw of the Netherlands, who was still alive. Edith, herself an Auschwitz survivor, grew up with Fritz in Vienna and is possibly the closest person alive who knew Fritz. Sarah and Scott contacted Edith but got no reply. If she had passed on, or changed address, Adam was unaware; the families were no longer in contact. In a last-ditch attempt to locate Edith, a search announcement was placed in the *Auschwitz Blad* (Bulletin). It worked. Edith, very much alive, noticed the announcement and contacted Sarah and Scott. She could not believe that somebody was looking for her. Fritz Zweigenthal, she confirmed, was indeed her "blood cousin." Edith, feeling now like "a voice out of the past" with this search request, said she did not know exactly what happened to her cousin Fritz.[8] What she did know, however, like the rest of Fritz's relatives, was that he did not survive the Holocaust; neither she nor any family members ever heard from him again.

With this contact, Sarah and Scott believed, they could close the case of Fritz Zweigenthal. Though family members did not know his exact place of death, it was clear he had not survived the war. However, as the adage goes, it's not over 'til it's over. Within a year of contact with Edith (Klaber) DeZeeuw, Sarah and Scott received a letter from a Robert Altschuler, of Metuchen, New Jersey: "Today I received an inquiry from Edith Klaber DeZeeuw in Holland about Fritz Zweigenthal. First of all I want to tell you my connection with Fritz. My mother Henriette and Fritz were first cousins. His mother and my grandmother were sisters."[9] Then this newly discovered relative of Fritz reported something startling: "As far as I know my mother received a card from Fritz mailed from Syria [to Kibbutz Ashdod Yakov in Palestine, not far from the Syrian border where we were living] around 1940. I believe that he served in the French Foreign Legion and was stationed there, and was planning to visit us. He never did. This was the last time we heard from him." For a while Robert Altschuler breathed new life into the Zweigenthal case (especially since he sent a photograph of Fritz Zweigenthal—the first and only known to Sarah and Scott). However, in the end, the operative phrase in Robert's note was "this was the last time we heard from him."

Fritz Zweigenthal (seated, front center) with his mother's cousins, Kaltenlaut Geben, Austria, c. 1930. (USHMM, courtesy of Robert Altschuler)

Though Robert Altschuler's information was qualitatively different than those of his family members—and with an interesting twist—the bottom line remained the same: Fritz Zweigenthal was never heard from again after the Holocaust and his last known location was an internment camp in France in 1941. Having gone as far as they could, Sarah and Scott have finally rested the case of Fritz Zweigenthal, together with those of the remaining 936 *St. Louis* passengers who preceded alphabetically on the passenger list.

Though accompanied by chance and uncertainty, and constrained by distance and time, the sojourns of Sarah and Scott took them from Washington Heights to the Golan Heights; from the cemeteries of Brussels to street corners in Tel Aviv; and to dozens of archives and libraries at various locations in between. In searching for the clues on the fates of the unaccounted-for passengers, they have spoken to many people—in person or through letters and e-mail.

What became clear was that when one searches for the fates of individuals from sixty years ago, there is no absolute end—the more testimony, the more facts, though at the same time the more complications. However, it can now be said that the fates and stories of the 937 *St. Louis* passengers—some more rich in detail than others—have been accounted for.

Afterword

Our research project to document the wartime experiences of each individual passenger provided the foundation for this publication. The bulk of the data establishing a passenger's fate came from primary sources or indices to primary sources. These include arrest, deportation, and death records for wartime Belgium, France, and the Netherlands; concentration camp registers; immigration and naturalization files; and the Social Security Death Benefits Index, among others. However, as the narrative of this book makes clear, in order to determine the fate of *all* the passengers, we had to address many gaps in the written record. Thus, there are a number of cases where we had to rely on information gleaned from interviews with survivors and their family members as well as other testimonial sources. We made every effort to independently verify this information; however, this was not always possible.

In tracing the fate of the passengers, our overriding goal was to document each path until the individual reached a place of safety, or, in the case of those passengers who came under Nazi control, until we could determine whether the person survived the war or died in a concentration camp or killing center.

Of the 620 *St. Louis* passengers who returned to continental Europe, we determined that eighty-seven were able to emigrate before Germany invaded western Europe on May 10, 1940.[1] Two hundred and fifty-four passengers in Belgium, France and the Netherlands after that date died during the Holocaust. Most of these people were murdered in the killing centers of Auschwitz and Sobibór; the rest died in internment camps, in hiding, or attempting to evade the Nazis. Three hundred and sixty five of the 620 passengers who returned to continental Europe survived the war. Of the 288 passengers sent to Britain, the vast majority were alive at war's end.

Around half of the original 937 passengers are known to have eventually migrated to the United States. In addition to the United States, passengers also made their way to Argentina, Australia, the Bahamas, Bolivia, Brazil, Canada, Chile, Colombia, Cuba, the Dominican Republic, Ecuador, Israel, Mexico, South Africa, Uruguay, and Venezuela. (Some of those destinations were simply wartime way stations.) About twenty continued their lives in continental Europe.

For a list of names of all 937 passengers, please see page 197. For basic information about a passenger's date and place of birth as well as additional information about the fate of the passenger and valuable resources about the *St. Louis*, go to www.ushmm .org/stlouis. We have made this information available via the internet to provide a complete accounting of the passengers' fates and to allow the entries to be updated with any new data that results from the publication of this book. Inquiries or information may be addressed to stlouis@ushmm.org.

Notes

Chapter 1. A Mystery Beckons

1. As of 2006, the Registry database contains more than 195,000 entries. The Registry staff handles approximately 34,000 requests annually. Survivors can be registered posthumously, allowing people to confirm if someone they knew survived the Holocaust even if they are not alive today. Registration forms are available in seventeen languages and can be obtained on the Museum's website, www.ushmm.org/registry.

2. Sarah Ogilvie was made director of the Registry in December 1997. She held that position until June 2000, at which point she was appointed the USHMM's director of education.

3. All of Clark Blatteis's quotations come from the audio oral history on deposit in the collection of the USHMM.

4. Morocco was under the control of the French Vichy government through 1942. Jewish refugees suffered discrimination and internment both before and after Vichy representatives surrendered to the Allies following the invasion of North Africa.

5. Arthur Morse, *While Six Million Died* (New York: Hart Publishing Co., 1967), 287.

6. Gordon Thomas and Max Morgan-Witts, *Voyage of the Damned,* 2nd ed. (Stillwater, Minn.: Motorbooks International, 1994), 234, 238.

Chapter 2. Fateful Voyage

1. All dollar amounts are in 1939 dollars.

2. Quoted in Thomas and Witts, *Voyage of the Damned,* 64. Schröder did not sail again after 1940. He is today honored at Yad Vashem as a "Righteous Among the Nations." As of the printing of this book,

Schröder is the only person who acted before the outbreak of World War II to be given that honor.

3. All Clark Blatteis quotations come from the audio interview on deposit in the collection of the USHMM.

4. "Journey from Hell and Back," *Washington Post*, Apr. 30, 1999.

5. Quoted in Thomas and Witts, *Voyage of the Damned*, 93.

6. Ibid., 81.

7. Ibid., 121.

8. Wilco de Vries's interview of Herta Fink-Hartig, Sept. 14, 1988, collection 3702, Herinneringscentrum kamp Westerbork, the Netherlands. Translation USHMM.

9. "No Harbor," *Jewish News of Greater Phoenix*, Nov. 27, 1998.

10. Liesl Joseph Loeb interview, Yad Vashem Archives, collection O.3/5706 (transcript) and collection O.33/1659 (archive cassette).

11. Berenson was an attorney well connected with the Cuban army chief Fulgencio Batista and a former president of the Cuban American Chamber of Commerce.

12. Josef Joseph Diary, courtesy Liesl Joseph Loeb.

13. Ogilvie and Miller's interview with Liesl Joseph Loeb, USHMM Archives. CNN interview with Loeb, May 1999.

14. Herta Fink-Hartig interview, September 14, 1988.

15. "Journey from Hell and Back."

16. Jews from Germany who wanted to immigrate to the United States had to apply for a visa at the nearest American consulate. There were numerous barriers to overcome. On the German side, the Nazis imposed the Reich Flight Tax, which left many emigrants impoverished. On the American side, the total number of immigrants allowed into the country each year was 163,000 for the entire world. American consuls were given wide latitude in evaluating affidavits of financial support and in interpreting requirements for admission. Each individual whose application was accepted was assigned a waiting number until the quota was filled for the year. Refugees could not leave for the United States until their waiting number came up; that is, until the refugees with lower numbers had arrived in the United States. Most *St. Louis* passengers had chosen to sail to Havana to get out of danger's way until their waiting number came up.

17. American public opinion overwhelmingly favored immigration restrictions. A *Fortune* magazine poll conducted shortly before the *St. Louis* incident indicated 83 percent of Americans opposed relaxing restrictions on immigration.

18. According to American Jewish JDC representative Cecilia Rokovsky, there were more than forty ships still on the water at the time the *St. Louis* was off the shores of Miami.

19. Secretary of State Cordell Hull and President Roosevelt were

aware of the plight of the passengers and decided not to intervene. See report of Coert du Bois, U.S. Consul General, Havana, June 7, 1939, State CDF 837.55J/39, where he states that Warren "went on to say that under no circumstances and in spite of considerable pressure would he or the Secretary of State or the President give me or the American Ambassador in Havana any instructions to intervene in the matter of the landing of the *St. Louis* refugees."

20. "Journey from Hell and Back."

Chapter 3. Kaddish

1. The key reference works Sarah initially consulted were Serge Klarsfeld, *Memorial to the Jews Deported from France 1942–1944* (New York: B. Klarsfeld Foundation, 1983; Paris: B. Klarsfeld Foundation, 1978); Serge Klarsfeld and Maxine Steinberg, *Memorial to the Jews Deported from Belgium 1942–1944* (New York: B. Klarsfeld Foundation, 1982); and *In Memoriam,* a listing of Jews deported from Holland.

2. These are published in the reference work *Death Books from Auschwitz* (Munich: K.G. Saur, 1995).

Chapter 4. Archives, Answers, and Anomalies

1. Founded in 1914 to assist Jews caught in the throes of World War I, the JDC has aided millions of Jews in more than eighty-five countries.

2. "Journey from Hell and Back."

3. Unless otherwise noted, all Herbert Karliner quotes come from Joe Unger's interview with Herbert Karliner, Feb. 18, 1985, part of Southeastern Florida Holocaust Memorial Center's oral history project. Copy of video interview in the archives of the USHMM.

4. "Journey from Hell and Back."

5. The Iron Guard massacred 120 Bucharest Jews in 1941 and a few thousand were deported to Transnistria in 1942.

Chapter 5. The First Israeli Survivor

1. This and all of Miller's quotes, unless otherwise indicated, are from Miller's e-mail to Edward J. Renehan Jr., July 10, 2003, USHMM Archives.

2. E-mail from Michael Barak to Miller, Apr. 3, 1997, USHMM Archives.

3. Miller's notes on telephone conversation with Michael Barak, Apr. 3, 1997, USHMM Archives.

4. Manfred Fink to Heinz Fink, July 28, 1939, courtesy of Michael Barak.

5. Manfred Fink to Heinz Fink, Nov. 13, 1939, courtesy of Michael Barak.

6. Miller's notes from an interview with Michael Barak, Mar. 2000, USHMM Archives.

Chapter 6. A Total American

1. Transcript of NPR *Weekend Edition* broadcast, Sept. 5, 1998.

2. Unless otherwise specified, all of Gerri Felder's comments are from her videotaped interview, USHMM Archive. Rudi Dingfelder's Auschwitz prisoner number was 174714.

3. Letter from Rudi Dingfelder to Isaac Felder, Gouda, Holland, Aug. 11, 1945, USHMM Archives.

4. Molly Abramowitz's notes of telephone conversation with David Donovan, May 15, 2001, USHMM Archives. Bob Felder told a version of this story to his family. According to the "family version," Rudi and five fellow prisoners escaped during the march near Schwerin. Three were shot in flight. Rudi and a French prisoner survived, and together they met up with American soldiers the following morning. The soldiers gave Rudi and his friend something to eat and then brought them to a nearby Allied military hospital, where the Frenchman eventually died.

5. Molly Abramowitz's notes on telephone conversation with Les Felder, May 8, 2001, USHMM Archives.

6. The family name of these people was Kolenbrander.

7. Molly Abramowitz's notes on telephone conversation with Gerri Felder, May 1, 2001, USHMM Archives; videotaped interview with Gerri Felder.

8. Rudi Dingfelder's name change to Robert Felder was formalized in Detroit on July 1, 1952, the day Bob became a U.S. citizen, as part of the naturalization process and paperwork.

9. Videotaped interview with Gerri Felder.

Chapter 7. It Depends What You Mean by "Survived"

1. Miller's notes on telephone conversation with Dr. Ellen Payner, Cleveland, Ohio, Aug. 1998; Edward J. Renehan Jr.'s notes of conversation with Dr. Ellen Payner, Sept. 15, 2003, both found in USHMM Archives.

Chapter 8. Reluctant Witness

1. Miller's notes on telephone conversation with unnamed informant, Nov. 25, 1998, USHMM Archives.

2. Miller's notes on telephone conversation with "Bela," Nov. 25, 1998, USHMM Archives.

Chapter 9. Shadows

1. E-mail from Martin Goldsmith to Miller, Aug. 1998, USHMM Archives. Martin Goldsmith has written of his family's Holocaust history in a remarkable book, *The Inextinguishable Symphony: A True Story of Love and Music in Nazi Germany* (New York: John Wiley & Sons, 2000).

2. Providing employment for the more than eight thousand Jewish musicians, singers, and actors expelled from German orchestras, opera companies, and theater groups during the 1930s, the Kulturbund allowed Jewish artists to perform for Jewish audiences. It was also used by the Nazis as a powerful propaganda tool to show the world how well Jews were supposedly being treated under the Third Reich.

3. Goldsmith, *The Inextinguishable Symphony*, 87.

4. Martin Goldsmith interview, *MacNeil-Lehrer Newshour*, Nov. 21, 2000.

5. Ibid.

6. Alex Goldschmidt to Gunther and Rosemarie Goldsmith, June 19, 1941. All letters quoted in this chapter are from Martin Goldsmith's *The Indistinguishable Symphony: A True Story of Music and Love in Nazi Germany* (New York: Wiley, 2000).

7. Alex Goldschmidt to Gunther and Rosemarie Goldsmith, no date.

8. Alex Goldschmidt to Gunther and Rosemarie Goldsmith, Sept. 22, 1941.

9. Alex Goldschmidt to Gunther and Rosemarie Goldsmith, Jan. 2, 1942.

10. Helmut Goldschmidt to Gunther and Rosemarie Goldsmith, Mar. 1942.

11. Alex Goldschmidt to Gunther and Rosemarie Goldsmith, May 9, 1942.

12. Helmut Goldschmidt to Gunther and Rosemarie Goldsmith, June 9, 1942.

Chapter 10. Frankfurt-on-the-Hudson

1. For an interesting account of the German Jewish community in Washington Heights, see Steven M. Lowenstein, *Frankfurt-on-the-Hudson* (Detroit: Wayne State University Press, 1989).

2. Miller's notes on interview with Rev. Walter Hes, Dec. 29, 1998, USHMM Archives.

3. Ogilvie and Miller's notes on telephone interview with Victoria Rosenberg, March 1999, USHMM Archives.

4. Ogilvie and Miller's notes on interview with Victoria Rosenberg, March 1999, USHMM Archives.

5. Ogilvie and Miller's notes on telephone interview with Meinhardt Hammerschlag, March 1999, USHMM Archives.

6. Ogilvie and Miller's notes on interview with Herbert Harwitt, March 1999, USHMM Archives.

7. Ogilvie and Miller's notes on interview with Eva Knoller, Feb. 1999, USHMM Archives; Edward J. Renehan Jr.'s notes on interview with Eva Knoller, May 2003, USHMM Archives.

8. Ogilvie and Miller's notes on telephone interview with Cynthia Muenz, April 1999, USHMM Archives.

Chapter 11. Graveyards

1. I. A. Lederman letter to Miller, Jan. 1999, USHMM Archives.

2. Gerda Waldbaum letter to Miller, Feb. 1999, USHMM Archives.

Chapter 12. Cruel Calculus

1. Miller's notes of telephone conversation with Marianne Meyerhoff, June 10, 1999, USHMM Archives.

2. Letter from Willie Dublon to the Heiman family, Apr. 2, 1940, USHMM Archives.

Chapter 13. Washington Heights Portrait: The Fortunate

1. In addition to these twenty-two Jewish passengers, six non-Jews—four Spanish and two Cuban nationals—were permitted to disembark.

2. All Meta Bonne quotes come from one of three sources, each housed in USHMM Archives: Miller's notes of interview with Ms. Bonne, May 1999; a videotaped interview with Ms. Bonne conducted by Miller and Ogilvie, May 2002; and notes from Ms. Bonne's May 2003 conversation with Edward J. Renehan Jr.

Chapter 14. Washington Heights Portrait: Exile in America

1. Unless otherwise indicated, all Ilse Marcus quotations come from one of three sources, all found in USHMM Archives: Miller's notes from his various encounters with Ms. Marcus since 1998; Ms. Marcus's videotaped interview with Miller and Ogilvie in March 2002; and Ilse's interview with Edward J. Renehan Jr., May 2, 2003.

2. At some point during the early summer of 1942, Kurt Marcus was transferred from Gurs to the Drancy transit camp in France. Convoy 25 departed for Auschwitz on August 28. The convoy carried one thousand Jews, 280 of them children under the age of seventeen, and arrived at Auschwitz on August 31. Upon arrival, 676 people, one of them most likely Kurt Marcus, were sent directly to the gas chambers. Berthold Meyer left France on Convoy 50, which departed Gurs on March 4, 1943. The destination of the convoy was Majdanek in Poland, where Berthold died. As for Ernst Meyer, he was deported from France on Convoy 18, which left Drancy for Auschwitz on August 12, 1942. Of the 942 people on the train, 705 were immediately gassed after the convoy arrived at its destination on August 14. It is believed that Ernst was one of that number.

Chapter 15. Sowing in Tears

1. The kibbutz is named in honor of Rabbi Eliyahu Gutmacher (1796–1875), one of the first to raise the call for religious Zionism.
2. Letter from Adolf Gruenthal, May 28, 1939, Gruenthal Family Papers, USHMM Archives.
3. Letter from Adolf Gruenthal, June 11, 1939, Gruenthal Family Papers, USHMM Archives.
4. Letter from Adolf Gruenthal, June 25, 1939, Gruenthal Family Papers, USHMM Archives.
5. Letter from Eva Willenz, July 25, 1998, Gruenthal Family Papers, USHMM Archives. Ogilvie and Miller have been unable to confirm, by way of archival documents, Lutz's and Horst Martin's eventual presence at Bergen-Belsen. Nevertheless, they were able to determine that the two boys were deported to Auschwitz.
6. Yehudit Silber interview, Mar. 9, 2000, USHMM Archives.
7. Ruth Gruenthal interview, Mar. 9, 2000, USHMM Archives.

Chapter 16. States of Insecurity

1. Ogilvie and Miller failed to verify a Richard Blum listed after the war in the publication *Sharit Ha-Platah* as a survivor in Trnava, Italy, as the Richard Blum of the *St. Louis*. And another Richard Blum—deported to Auschwitz on August 8, 1942—at first looked like a match until birthdates were compared. The Blum who died at Auschwitz had been born April 23, 1883, not August 28, 1886.
2. Letter to Miller from Batya Unterschatz, Feb. 1998, USHMM Archives.
3. E-mail to Miller from Batya Unterschatz, Jan. 2000, USHMM Archives.

4. Miller's notes from interview with Batya Unterschatz, Mar. 2000, USHMM Archives.

5. Miller's notes on telephone interview with Hanan Blum, Mar. 2000, USHMM Archives.

6. Miller's notes of interview with Hanan Blum, June 2001, USHMM Archives.

7. E-mail to Miller from Seev Blum, courtesy of Seev Blum, USHMM Archives, February 24, 2003.

8. Letter from Betty Blum to Seev Blum, courtesy of Seev Blum, USHMM Archives, April 6, 1939.

9. Letter from Betty Blum to Seev Blum, courtesy of Seev Blum, USHMM Archives, July 19, 1939.

10. Letter from Betty Blum to [Brauns], courtesy of Seev Blum, USHMM Archives, January 1945.

Chapter 17. Displaced Persons

1. Letter from Hannelore Grünberg-Klein to Miller, Nov. 1998, USHMM Archives.

2. Miller's notes of telephone conversation with Hannelore Grünberg-Klein, May 2001.

3. Miller's notes of conversation with Mrs. Fanto, Hoboken, N.J., Apr. 1, 1999, USHMM Archives.

4. It seems likely the Jewish Fantos may be descendants of Sephardic Jews from Spain who fled to central or eastern Europe following the Spanish Inquisition and the expulsion of 1492.

5. Miller's notes of conversation with Elizabeth Bergstein, New York, Apr. 2, 1999, USHMM Archives. Also Edward J. Renehan Jr. notes of conversation with Elizabeth Bergstein, New York, Sept. 12, 2003, USHMM Archives.

Chapter 18. Kew Gardens Portrait

1. All Judith Steel quotes come from interviews with Museum researchers; Miller's notes, July 2001, and Renehan's notes, May 1, 2003, USHMM Archives.

2. Judith's parents boarded a train to the Drancy transit camp just days after they gave their little girl to the OSE. From Drancy, they and 1,001 other Jews traveled to Auschwitz on Convoy 33, which departed the station at Le Bourget/Drancy on September 16, 1942, at 8:55 A.M. Two days later, when the train arrived at its destination, the Germans selected 147 women and 300 men for forced labor. Guards marched the remainder of the convoy—556 people in all—directly to the gas chambers.

At the end of the war, just thirty-eight of the original total of 1,003 Jews from Convoy 33 survived. There is no record of Joseph or Irmgard making it past initial selection at Auschwitz on September 18.

Chapter 19. The Missing

1. U.S. Immigration and Naturalization Service letter to Miller, Jan. 18, 2000, USHMM Archives.

2. Letter from Ruth Heilbrun to Miller, Aug. 6, 1998, USHMM Archives. The Mosers referred to here and in the following note are another *St. Louis* passenger family, of no relation to Rosalie Moser.

3. Miller's notes of conversation with Herbert Karliner, Aug. 3, 1998, USHMM Archives.

4. Archives communales de Périgeux. Documents sent to Museum by Diane Afoumado, Oct. 2003.

5. Archives départementales de Dordogne. Document sent to Museum by Diane Afoumado, Dec. 2003.

6. Archives, town hall of Salagnac. Document sent to Museum by Polly Haas, June 2004.

7. Molly Abramowitz's notes of conversation with Adam Klaber, Jan. 2002, USHMM Archives.

8. Letter from Edith (Klaber) DeZeeuw to USHMM, Mar. 30, 2003, USHMM Archives.

9. Letter from Robert Altschuler to USHMM, Apr. 14, 2003, USHMM Archives.

Afterword

1. The number may actually be higher as there are some passengers for whom no specific date of emigration is available; they were excluded from this count. One additional passenger, as has been noted previously, was not a refugee.

Index

The St. Louis *Passengers*

The 937 names on this list come from a Cuban Immigration Department/ Hamburg-America Line manifest held by the American Jewish Joint Distribution Committee archive in New York.

Aber, Evelyn	Bach, Willy	Bibo, Günther
Aber, Renate	Back, Cecilia	Biener, Elsa
Aberbach, Adolf	Back, James	Biener, Selmar
Aberbach, Anna	Bajor, Ladislas	Blachmann, Arthur
Ackermann, Bertha	Bak, Stella Bianca	Blachmann, Erna
Adelberg, Samuel	Ball, Magdalena	Blachmann, Gerda
Adler, Berthold	Ball, Rudolf	Blatteis, Ernst
Adler, Carola	Banemann, Jeanette	Blatteis, Gerda
Adler, Chaskel	Banemann, Margit	Blatteis, Klaus
Adler, Paul	Banemann, Philipp	Blaut, Arnold
Adler, Regina	Bardeleben, Anna	Blaut, Artur
Adler, Resi	Bardeleben, Marianne	Blechner, Oskar
Alexander, Gisela	Baruch, Frieda	Blum, Betty
Alexander, Karl	Baruch, Ludwig	Blum, Richard
Alexander, Leo	Begleiter, Alfred	Blumenstein, Elsa
Altschiller, Jütte	Begleiter, Naftali	Blumenstein, Heinz-Georg
Altschul, Gerd	Begleiter, Sara	Blumenstein, Regi
Altschul, Hans	Beifus, Alfred	Blumenstock, Lea
Altschul, Lotte	Beifus, Emma	Blumenstock, Mechel
Altschul, Rolf	Bendheim, Bertha	Blumenstock, Ruth
Apfel, Babette	Bendheim, Ludwig	Boas, Benno
Arens, Alfred	Benjamin, Adelheid	Boas, Charlotte
Arndt, Arthur	Berggrün, Antonie	Bohm, Heinz
Arndt, Hertha	Berggrün, Ludwig	Bohm, Kurt
Arndt, Lieselotte	Bergmann, Otto	Bonne, Beatrice
Aron, Alfred	Bergmann, Rosy	Bonne, Hans-Jacob
Aron, Sofie	Bernstein, Bruno	Bonne, Meta
Ascher, Herbert	Bernstein, Julius	Borchardt, Alice
Ascher, Vera	Bernstein, Margot	Borchardt, Heinrich
Atlas, Charlotte	Bernstein, Selma	Bornstein, Wilhelm

197

Brandt, Dieter
Brandt, Johannes
Brandt, Lina
Brann, Alfred
Brauer, Erich
Brauer, Käthe
Breitbarth, Arthur
Brenner, Blanka
Broderova, Elizabeth
Brück, Herbert
Brühl, Hedwig
Brühl, Lieselotte
Brühl, Walter
Buchholz, Auguste
Buchholz, Wilhelm
Buff, Fritz
Bukofzer, Martha
Buxbaum, Levi
Camnitzer, Edith
Camnitzer, Rosalie
Camnitzer, Siegfried
Chaim, Georg
Chraplewski, Jan
Chraplewski, Klara
Chraplewski, Peter
Chraplewski, Siegfried
Cohen, Rudolf
Cohn, Eugen
Cohn, Georg
Cohn, Helene
Cohn, Johanna
Cohn, Lewis
Cohn, Lydia
Cohn, Rita
Cohn, Sara
Cohn, Walter
Cohnstaedt, Fritz
Cohnstaedt, Nelly
Collin, Auguste
Cunow, Carl
Czerninski, Hilde
Czerninski, Inge
Czerninski, Max
Daniel, Anna
Danziger, Karl
Danziger, Rosa
David, Emma
Dingfelder, Johanna
Dingfelder, Leopold
Dingfelder, Rudi
Donath, Paul
Dörnberg, Gertha

Dresel, Alfred
Dresel, Richard
Dresel, Ruth
Dresel, Zilla
Dubiecki, Bajrech
Dubiecki, Bella
Dubiecki, Golda
Dublon, Erich
Dublon, Erna Dora
Dublon, Eva
Dublon, Lore
Dublon, Willi-Otto
Dzialowski, Bruno
Dzialowski, Lici
Eckmann, Egon
Edelstein, Ida
Eichwald, Fritz
Einhorn, Aron
Einhorn, Gitel
Eisner, Ludwig
Epstein, Bettina
Epstein, Moritz
Erdmann, Rosa
Erdmann, Simon
Eskenazy, Albert
Eskenazy, Gertrud
Eskenazy, Nissin
Falk, Eugen
Falkenstein, Hilde
Falkenstein, Max
Fanto, Julius
Feig, Werner
Feilchenfeld, Alice
Feilchenfeld, Bertha Judith
Feilchenfeld, Henny
Feilchenfeld, Rafael
Feilchenfeld, Wolf
Fink, Herta
Fink, Manfred
Fink, Michael
Finkelstein, Ina
Fischbach, Amalia Dull
Fischbach, Amalie Fishback
Fischbach, Jonas
Fischbach, Moritz
Fischer, Hans-Hermann
Fischer, Johanna
Fischer, Ruth
Flamberg, Brandla
Flamberg, Fella
Frank, Clara
Frank, Manfred

Frank, Max
Frank, Moritz
Frank, Siegfried
Frank, Ursula
Fränkel, Alice
Fränkel, Hans
Fränkel, Leo
Frankfurter, Lilly
Freiberg, Gisela
Freiberg, Herta
Freiberg, Ruda Regina
Freund, Lieselotte
Freund, Philipp
Freund, Therese
Fried, Engelbert
Friedemann, Walter
Friedheim, Alfred
Friedheim, Edith
Friedheim, Hertha
Friedmann, Amalie
Friedmann, Bruno
Friedmann, Georg
Friedmann, Lilian
Friedmann, Rose
Friedmann, Ruth
Friedmann, Willy
Fröhlich, Max
Fuchs-Marx, Anna
Fuchs-Marx, Walter
Fuld, Hans
Fuld, Julie
Fuld, Ludwig,
Gabel, Beate
Gabel, Gerhard
Gabel, Heinrich
Gelband, Benjamin
Gelband, Chana
Gembitz, Heinz-Adolf
Gembitz, Martha
Gembitz, Max
Gerber, Rosa
Gerber, Ruth
Glade, Bruno
Glaser, Arthur
Glaserfeld, Moritz Max
Glass, Herbert
Glücksmann, Hans Heinrich
Glücksmann, Heinrich
Glücksmann, Margarete
Goldbaum, Anna
Goldberg, Wilhelm
Goldreich, Rudolf

Goldreich, Therese
Goldschmidt, Adolf
Goldschmidt, Alex
Goldschmidt, Else
Goldschmidt, Fritz
Goldschmidt, Gerda
Goldschmidt, Inge
Goldschmidt, Klaus-Helmut
Goldschmidt, Lore
Goldstein, Heinz
Goldstein, Hermann
Goldstein, Recha
Gottfeld, Julius
Gottfeld, Rosa
Gotthelf, Fritz
Gotthelf, Käte
Gottlieb, Sali
Gottschalk, Charlotte
Gottschalk, Erika
Gottschalk, Jacob
Gottschalk, Regina
Greilsamer, Erich
Greve, Evelyn
Greve, Heinz Ludwig
Greve, Johanna
Greve, Walter
Gronowetter, Hermann
Gross, Frieda
Gross, Johanna
Grossmann, Erich
Grossmann, Friedrich
Grossmann, Helene
Grossmann, Henny
Grossmann, Idel
Groza de Quintero, Ileana
Gruber, Alex
Gruber, Gisela
Gruber, Hermann
Gruber, Max
Grubner, Jakob
Grubner, Joachim
Grubner, Mano
Grubner, Ryfka
Grünberg, Etty
Grünstein, Gerd Fritz
Grünstein, Heinz
Gruenthal, Adolf
Gruenthal, Bertha-Ellen
Gruenthal, Else
Gruenthal, Horst-Martin
Gruenthal, Lutz
Gruenthal, Margarete

Gruenthal, Ruthild
Gruenthal, Sibyll
Gruenthal, Walter
Gutmann, Martha
Guttmann, Harry
Guttmann, Helga
Guttmann, Josef
Guttmann, Margarete
Guttmann, Rosi
Guttmann, Ruth
Guttmann, Sally
Haas, Anton
Haas, Elisabeth
Haas, Leo
Haber, Nathan
Hamburger, Arthur
Hammerschlag, Max
Hammerschlag, Moses
Händler, Fritz
Händler, Georg
Händler, Marie
Händler, Rosamunde
Hausdorff, Arthur
Hausdorff, Gertrud
Hauser, Cecilie
Hauser, Hermann
Hecht, Charlotte
Heidt, Else
Heidt, Fritz
Heilbrun, Berna
Heilbrun, Bruno
Heilbrun, Günther
Heilbrun, Ingeborg
Heilbrun, Johanna
Heilbrun, Leon
Heilbrun, Norbert
Heilbrun, Ruth
Heilbrun, Sally
Heim, Emil
Heim, Gerda
Heimann, Bella
Heimann, Erwin
Heinemann, Hilmar
Heldenmuth, Alfred
Heldenmuth, Lilo
Heldenmuth, Selma
Heller, Frantisek
Heller, Freide
Heller, Irma
Heller, Moritz
Hermann, Gerda
Hermann, Julius

Hermann, Sophie
Hermanns, Julius
Herrmann, Fritz
Herz, Amalie
Herz, Anna
Herz, Max
Herz, Walter
Hess, Adolf
Hess, Ilse
Hess, Jette
Hess, Martin
Hess, Vera
Hesse, Robert
Heymann, Arno
Heymann, Dorothea
Heymann, Hedwig
Hilb, Fritz
Hirsch, Hermann
Hirsch, Joachim
Hirsch, Margot
Hirsch, Max
Hirschberg, Julius
Hirschberg, Regina
Hirschfeld, Ruth
Hirschfeld, Siegfried
Hoffmann, Emma
Hoffmann, Karl
Hoffmann, Selma
Hofmann, Cilly
Hofmann, Siegfried
Hopp, Margarethe
Huber, Lilli
Hüneberg, Walter
Isakowski, Kurt
Isner, Babette
Isner, Bella
Isner, Justin
Isner, Ruth
Israel, Hugo
Jacobowitz, Martin
Jacobowitz, Mathilde
Jacobowitz, Walter
Jacobsohn, Erich
Jacobsohn, Margarete
Jacobsohn, Thomas
Jacoby, Käthe
Jacoby, Otto
Jacoby, Regina
Jacoby, Susanna
Jimenez, José
Joel, Günther
Joel, Johanna

May, Ludwig
Mayer, Adalbert
Mayer, Fanny
Mayer, Ludwig
Mayer, Samuel
Mendel, Christine
Mendel, Elisabeth
Mendel, Karl
Menendez, Mercedes
Menendez, Ramira
Menendez, Zeza
Messinger, Pessla
Messinger, Salo
Messinger, Selman
Metis, Annette
Metis, Lotte
Metis, Wolfgang
Meyer, Anna
Meyer, Berthold
Meyer, Elfriede
Meyer, Ernst
Meyer, Joseph
Meyer, Stephanie
Meyerhoff, Charlotte
Meyerstein, Alice
Meyerstein, Hans
Meyerstein, Ludwig
Michaelis, Cecilie
Michaelis, Walter
Moser, Edmund
Moser, Rosalie
Moses, Alfred
Moses, Eugen
Moses, Georg
Moses, Helmut
Moses, Martha
Moses, Thea
Moskiewicz, Ismar
Motulsky, Arno
Motulsky, Lia
Motulsky, Lothar
Motulsky, Rena
Mück, Joachim
Mühlenthal, Charlotte
Müller, Ernst
Müller, Margot
Muenz, Karl
Muenz, Meta
Muenz, Paula
Muenz, Sophie
Nathanson, Harry
Nathanson, Hilde Nora

Neuberg, Ilse
Neuberg, Wilhelm
Neufeld, Fritz
Neufeld, Joseph
Neuhaus, Felix
Oberdorfer, Gerda
Oberdorfer, Hedwig
Oberdorfer, Margarete
Oberdorfer, Max
Oberdorfer, Simon
Oberdorfer, Stefanie
Oberndorfer, Paula
Obstfeld, Hermine
Oehl, Dorothea
Oehl, Käthe
Oppé, Armin
Oppé, Margarethe
Oppenheimer, Adolf
Oppler, Arthur
Oppler, Elise
Ostrodzki, Betti
Ostrodzki, Ernst
Oyres, Herbert
Oyres, Karl
Pander, Berta
Pander, Hilde
Pander, Max
Philippi, Ernst
Philippi, Gert
Philippi, Margarete
Philippi, Wolfgang
Pick, Elisabeth
Pinthus, Heinz
Pommer, Martin
Präger, Margarethe
Präger, Siegfried
Preger, Alexander
Preiss, Gerhard
Preiss, Lisbeth
Quintero, Lazaro
Rabinowitz, Harry
Rebenfeld, Kurt
Recher, Irene
Recher, Moritz
Reichenteil, Betty
Reichenteil, Joseph
Reif, Chaje Leja
Reif, Friedrich
Reif, Liane
Reingenheim, Fanny
Reingenheim, Jacob
Reingenheim, Selma

Reutlinger, Elly
Reutlinger, Renate
Richter, Marianne
Riegelhaupt, Cypora
Riegelhaupt, Israel
Riesenburger, Hermann
Ring, Erich
Ring, Erna
Ring, Jacques
Rinteln, Elisabeth
Rinteln, Walter
Ritter, Wilhelm
Rosenbach, Heinz
Rosenbaum, Rosa
Rosenberg, Louis
Rosenberg, Ricka
Rosenberg, Selig
Rosenfeld, Hans
Rosenfeld, Selma
Rosenfeld, Steffi
Rosenthal, Johanna
Rosenthal, Kurt
Rosenthal, Margrit
Rosenthal, Max
Rosenthal, Rolf
Rosenzweig, Siegfried
Ross, Heinrich
Roth, Camilla
Roth, Ernst
Roth, Harry
Rothmann, Jenny
Rothmann, Martin
Rotholz, Berthold
Rotholz, Guenther
Rotholz, Horst
Rotholz, Margarete
 Loewenstein
Rotholz, Margarete Spanier
Rotholz, Siegfried
Rothschild, Erwin
Rothschild, Eva
Rothschild, Frieda
Roubitschek, Ernst
Roubitschek, Pauline
Roubitschek, Richard
Ryndsionski, Ferdinand
Safier, Cypora
Safier, Eva
Safier, Jakob
Salm, Ida
Salm, Leopold
Salmon, Edith

Salmon, Egon
Salmon, Erna
Salomon, Moritz
Salomon, Sybilla
Sandberg, Delta
Sandberg, Ruth
Schafranik, Heinrich
Schafranik, Leontine
Schapira, Henriette
Schapira, Leib
Schelansky, Frieda
Schelansky, Hans Heinz
Scheuer, Gertrud
Scheyer, Martha
Schild, Irma
Schild, Ison
Schillinger, Georg Jezi
Schillinger, Jan
Schillinger, Marie
Schillinger, Samuel
Schlesinger, Frederike
Schlesinger, Max
Schlesinger, Meta
Schlesinger, Richard
Schoeps, Anni
Schoeps, Beate
Schoeps, Kurt
Schönberger, Moritz
Schönemann, Gertrud
Schönemann, Siegfried
Schönemann, Wolfgang
Schott, Else
Schott, Kurt
Schott, Siegfried
Schuck, Gertrud
Schüfftan, Therese
Schüfftan, Walter
Schüfftan, Wolfgang
Schulhof, Julius
Schulhof, Stella
Schumanovsky, Emil
Schwager, Albert
Schwager, Resi
Schwalbendorf, Josef
Schwartz, Oskar
Schwartz, Regina
Schweiger, Sofie
Schweitzer, Jenny
Schweitzer, Max,
Secemski, Aron
Secemski, Hanna
Secemski, Luise

Segal, Moses
Segal, Sabine
Seliger, Walter
Seligmann, Alma
Seligmann, Max
Seligmann, Rosa
Seligmann, Siegbert
Seligmann, Siegfried
Seligmann, Ursula
Siegel, Arthur
Sietz, Lea
Silber, Chaja
Silber, Leo
Silber, Salomon
Silberstein, Gert
Silberstein, Kurt
Silberstein, Renate
Silberstein, Thea
Silzer, Leontine
Silzer, Paul
Simon, Carl
Simon, Edith
Simon, Ilse
Simon, Martin
Simon, Rolf
Simon, Selma Katz
Simon, Selma Schlesinger
Singer, Amalie
Singer, Josef
Singer, Max
Siperstein, Josefine
Sklow, Betty
Skotzki, Charlotte
Skotzki, Günther
Skotzki, Helga
Skotzki, Inge
Spanier, Babette
Spanier, Fritz
Spanier, Ines
Spanier, Renate
Speier, Meier
Spira, Hanna
Spitz, Erich
Spitz, Ursula
Spitz, Vera
Springer, Julius
Srog, Abraham
Srog, Mathilde
Stahl, Rosa
Stark, Moses
Stark, Paul
Stark, Pessel

Stein, Else
Stein, Erich
Stein, Fanny
Stein, Grete
Stein, Joseph
Stein, Kurt
Stein, Mauritius
Stein, Werner
Sternberg, Alice
Sternlicht, Gertrud
Sternlicht, Lotte
Strauss, Alfons
Strauss, Emma
Strauss, Heinrich
Strauss, Hermann
Strauss, Josef
Strauss, Kurt
Strauss, Max
Sydower, Wilhelm
Tannenbaum, Karl
Tannenbaum, Malchen
Tichauer, Else
Tichauer, Herbert
Tischler, Harry
Tischler, Lina
Trödel, Blanca
Trödel, Erich
Trödel, Leopold
Trödel, Walter
Turkowicz, Edith
Turkowicz, Helene
Turkowicz, Joer
Unger, Bertha
Velman, Hilde
Velman, Walter
Vendig, Charlotte
Vendig, Ernst
Vendig, Fritz-Dieter
Vendig, Heiner
Vendig, Paulina
Wachtel, Amanda
Wachtel, Joseph
Waldbaum, Gerda
Waldbaum, Margarete
Waldbaum, Viktor
Wallerstein, Anton
Wallerstein, Edith
Wallerstein, Julius
Wallerstein, Paula
Warschawsky, Franz Peter
Warschawsky, Hans
Warschawsky, Johanna

Warschawsky, Ursula
Wartelski, Leo
Wassermann, Paula
Wasservogel, Irma
Wasservogel, Viktor
Wechselmann, Margarete
Wechselmann, Oskar
Weil, Anneliese
Weil, Arthur
Weil, Berthold
Weil, Clara
Weil, Eduard
Weil, Emma
Weil, Ernst
Weil, Felix
Weil, Gustav
Weil, Ingeborg
Weil, Julius
Weil, Susanna
Weil, Thekla
Weiler, Meier
Weiler, Recha
Weinberg, Walter

Weinstein, Dina
Weinstein, Siegfried
Weinstock, Arthur
Weinstock, Charlotte
Weinstock, Ernst
Weis, Bella
Weis, Max
Weisel, Friederike
Weiser, Chawa
Weiser, Ignaz
Weiss, Gerda
Weiss, Laja
Weiss, Leopold
Weiss, Majer
Weissler, Walter
Weisz, Samuel
Weltmann, Elly
Weltmann, Erich
Weltmann, Renate
Wertheim, Fritz
Westheimer, Klara
Wiesenfelder, Martin
Wilmersdörfer, Flora

Wilmersdörfer, Siegfried
Windmüller, Berta
Windmüller, Hans
Windmüller, Rudi
Windmüller, Salomon
Winkler, Istvan
Wolf, Abraham
Wolf, Elisabeth
Wolf, Johanna
Wolf, Lina
Wolf, Moritz
Wolfermann, Flora
Wolfermann, Jacob
Wolff, Adolf
Wolff, Else
Wolff, Hildegard
Wolff, Max
Zellner, Gertrud
Zellner, Margot
Zellner, Max
Zellner, Ruth
Zweigenthal, Fritz